Shreemad Bhagavad Gita: Verses & Translations

Bhakti Marga Publications

First Edition
ISBN: 978-3-940381-59-0
Printed in Germany

Bhakti Marga Publications
c/o Shree Peetha Nilaya
Am Geisberg 1-8, 65321 Heidenrod - Springen, Germany

publications@bhaktimarga.org
bhaktimarga.org

BHAKTI MARGA

Shreemad Bhagavad Gita

VERSES AND TRANSLATIONS

ABOUT BHAKTI MARGA

Founded in 2005 by Paramahamsa Sri Swami Vishwananda, Bhakti Marga, "the path of devotion", is a movement of universal Love that is spreading quickly throughout the world. Its headquarters near Frankfurt, Germany, has become a hub of spiritual activities, ranging from small courses and workshops to large festivals and events, including an annual "Just Love" Festival. This three-day event is held every summer and celebrates the joy of the spiritual path, the uplifting qualities of divine music, and the delight of being in community with other spiritual seekers.

Expanding internationally, Bhakti Marga temples and other devotional groups have blossomed around the globe. These groups give everyone access to Sri Swami Vishwananda's timeless teachings of Divine Love and devotion to God, as well as provide opportunities to connect with others on the spiritual path. Through books, CD's, YouTube videos, social media, livestreams and online courses, the mission of Bhakti Marga is growing and touching new hearts every day.

More information about Paramahamsa Vishwananda can be found at the end of this book and also by visiting **bhaktimarga.org.**

TABLE OF CONTENTS

INTRODUCTION

The *Shreemad Bhagavad Gita* (also called the *Bhagavad Gita* or just the *Gita*) has become the most popular, most read, most revered Hindu scripture in the world. Its name literally means 'Song of God' and its 700 verses are found within the epic 100,000-verse *Mahabharat* of the sage Veda Vyasa.

Organised into eighteen significant chapters, the *Bhagavad Gita* presents the timeless discourse held between Lord Krishna and the dejected and confused warrior Arjuna, just before the massive Kurukshetra War - the battle between the virtuous Pandavas and their greedy cousins, the Kauravas. Arjuna's questions and Krishna's answers reveal the deepest knowledge of the awareness of the Soul, and we listen in as the narrator, Sanjaya, describes the entire event to the blind king, Dhritarashtra.

In his extensive commentary found in the book *'Shreemad Bhagavad Gita - The Song of Love'*, Paramahamsa Sri Swami Vishwananda explains each verse of the *Gita* and its relevance to our spiritual growth. Ultimately, he says:

"When you start on your spiritual path, you have a battle: you perceive all the negative qualities within yourself more strongly. Sometimes you'll awaken a quality which has never been there before. But this is the purification, the Kurukshetra, that you go through. You uproot all these qualities one by one and transform them, until finally you have the Love of God that stays.

That's Realisation: to receive His Grace, to manifest His Love, and to beam His Love."

We can see this internal war reflected clearly in the *Gita*, as Arjuna struggles with what he knows to be right. We can all relate, as we also are on an endless search for happiness, trying to determine what is best and what is not, and trying to find and fulfil our purpose for being. Seeing it this way, human life on earth is truly a continual battle, internally and externally, between good and bad, right and wrong, and duality of all kinds.

Since it has always been Paramahamsa Vishwananda's wish to bring people from across the world together in the name of universal Love, he recommends reading the *Bhagavad Gita* as one way to move in that direction. In fact, it is so important to our progress, he recommends reading it every day, even if only one page a day. What does it do for us? Paramahamsa Vishwananda tells this story as an example:

A disciple asked his Guru, "How can I get quick Realisation?" And the Guru said, "Read the *Bhagavad Gita*." So he read the book and, when he finished, he went to the Master and asked, "Okay, I have finished... now what?" And the Master said, "Read it again and again and again and again." So after ten times, the disciple was bored and he asked, "Okay, I've read it ten times now and nothing has happened."

In reply, the Guru said, "Look..." and pointed to the corner. Sitting there was an old bucket that was dirty and rusty and full of holes. The Master told him, "Take that bucket and go to the river. Fill the bucket with water and bring it back here." So he did as he was told, but by the time he had arrived, all of the water was gone. Again the Master sent him to the river and again, the water leaked out and he had to start all over. He did this twenty times, and finally in frustration, he went to the Guru and said, "What's the point of this? I cannot bring water because there are so many holes in this bucket!" And the Master says, "Yes, but look at the bucket. Now it is clean, it is brilliant, it is magnificent. The light is shining from it."

So that is the point. The more you immerse yourself into the divine scriptures like the *Bhagavad Gita*, the more it will cleanse you. The more you are cleansed, the more the divine qualities will grow inside of you and the more the Divine Light will shine from within you.

In addition, he says that the eighteen chapters are symbolic of the eighteen days of the battle between the Kauravas and the Pandavas. He adds, "It is also said in the shastras that for someone who wishes to surrender to the Lord, it will take eighteen steps to fully surrender. One must go through these eighteen steps, step by step. [...] The greatness of the *Gita* is that at the end, whatever one wishes for with a pure heart, one will receive. Going through the *Gita*, the heart goes through a sieve and gets purified. The mind goes through transformation, and the soul is cleansed."

With that said, it is obvious that the *Bhagavad Gita* is much more than 'just a book'; it is a personal journey that will take us far beyond our limited expectations.

The book in your hands is comprised simply of the verses and translations of the *Bhagavad Gita* without commentary. This is done so that you can come to your own insights and listen to your heart as you read the sacred passages. You can then make your own connections to the issues in your daily life.

To begin, we have provided a simple "family tree" to help those new to the *Gita* keep track of who is related to who, and at the end, we have given a pronunciation guide to the Sanskrit for those who would like to chant the verses themselves.

However, before you begin, it still may be helpful to have an overview of each of the chapters, so that you can find your way along the journey of the "eighteen steps" to the Divine. The next few pages will give you a sense of the purpose of each chapter.

OVERVIEW: THE EIGHTEEN CHAPTERS OF THE BHAGAVAD GITA

In his commentary '*Shreemad Bhagavad Gita -The Song of Love*', Paramahamsa Vishwananda gives an overview of the entire *Bhagavad Gita*, revealing the purpose and the meaning of each chapter:

"The first chapter of the *Gita* is Arjuna Vishaada Yoga, the Dejection of Arjuna. Arjuna says, 'I can't even hold my bow in my hand, how will I fight?' Krishna says, 'Fight! This is your dharma! This is your duty!' Here you will see that Krishna is taking the role of the Guru. Krishna doesn't say, 'Oh, My dear, you are sad. Don't fight now! Let's go home!' [...] Krishna tells him, 'No, you can't leave, you have to fight!' Then Krishna gave the knowledge of the Self to Arjuna."

Paramahamsa Vishwananda further explains, "Through this drama, Krishna gives this knowledge to humanity, to every human being in this world. What Krishna teaches in the *Gita* is the essence of the *Vedas*, the *Puranas*, the *Upanishads*, the *Bible*, and the *Qur'an*: everything is present in it."

The second chapter is Sankhya Yoga, the knowledge of the Self. In this chapter, Krishna starts explaining to Arjuna the eternal qualities of the soul, and tells him again to fight and perform his duty. Krishna also explains to Arjuna what attitude he should take to perform his duty. Chapter 2 is often recognised as a summary of the entire *Gita* because it touches on all the different types of yoga which will be described in more detail in the later chapters.

The third chapter is Karma Yoga, which is about the power of action. It begins by Arjuna not understanding what his duty is. It is not clear to him whether Krishna wants him to renounce all action or to fight. Krishna starts to explain that there are two modes of spiritual practice one does to attain the Divine: Jyaana Yoga, the path of renunciation, and Karma Yoga, the path of action. In this chapter, Krishna says that as long as the mind is not purified, it does not matter whether one is sitting in a cave or fighting a battle. In both forms, one is bound by creation to perform. Therefore, Krishna tells Arjuna to perform Karma Yoga with the right attitude and do his duty. Likewise, for those that have not acquired the knowledge of the Self, before following the Jyaana Yoga path, they must purify the mind through action, Karma Yoga.

In the fourth chapter, Jyaana Vibhaaga Yoga, Krishna goes deeper into the power of knowledge, action and renunciation. After telling Arjuna that he should do his duty and purify the mind, Krishna starts talking about the awareness one should have while practicing Karma Yoga.

Krishna tells Arjuna that not only should one perform action with detachment, but one should also have the awareness of the Divine at all times while performing that action. The majority of the chapter deals with the attitude of surrender to the Divine. Krishna explains that all activities that humans do should be done as a sacrifice to the Lord. The chapter concludes by Krishna explaining the qualities one needs to have when performing one's actions, most importantly faith. Furthermore, Krishna also explains the importance of a spiritual teacher, a Guru, who can reveal the knowledge of the Self.

The fifth chapter is Karma Sannyasa Yoga. The word 'karma' is usually translated as 'action', but here in this chapter it is connected to the word 'sannyasa', so Karma Sannyasa Yoga is the yoga of the renunciation of action. Arjuna was unable to really understand what Krishna was trying to tell him in the previous chapters, and there was still plenty of doubt in Arjuna's mind. He was missing the key points that Krishna had outlined for him. So, Krishna explains to Arjuna why Karma Yoga is the best path for him. He also talks about how a Karma Yogi should act, the role God plays in the actions of man, and the qualities of a person who has achieved the goal of Karma Yoga. He concludes the chapter by telling Arjuna that one should practice Karma Yoga till one is completely free from desire, fear and anger. Karma Yoga as explained by Krishna is how one should perform all actions; it purifies the mind so that one can meditate on the Lord with a clear mind.

The sixth chapter is Dhyaana Yoga, about the power of meditation. In the beginning, before speaking about meditation, Krishna reiterates to Arjuna the importance of renouncing the thoughts of the world and transforming the mind from a lower state into a higher state of consciousness. Once one has achieved this state through Karma Yoga, one should then change the mind's focus from the outer reality to the inner reality.

The rest of the chapter talks about how to focus the attention inwardly through meditation. After hearing Krishna speak, Arjuna expresses doubt about his own ability to control the mind, since the mind is so restless. Krishna tells Arjuna that with constant practice and non-attachment one can control the mind. He also says that no effort is ever lost, one will eventually attain the Lord, in one life or the next. In the next six chapters, Krishna goes into more detail about the divine qualities of God that one should meditate upon.

The seventh chapter is Jyaana Vijyaana Yoga, the path of knowledge. In this chapter, Krishna will give Arjuna the knowledge of faith, the knowledge of how to dedicate oneself, and how to serve in order to attain Him. In the next few chapters, there is a radical shift, where we witness Krishna describing in detail who He is as the ultimate, personal deity. Now, we begin to see, in Krishna's own words, how the practice of Bhakti (devotion) can win a relationship with Him, and how through His Divine Grace we can attain Him and be saved from the never-ending cycle of birth and death.

The eighth chapter, Akshara Brahma Yoga, is about how to perceive and attain the ultimate reality, the Super Spirit. At the beginning of the *Bhagavad Gita*, Arjuna's mind was full of many questions. Even at this point in the story, we see that he still has questions. Arjuna is not yet fully realised, but his heart is opening. There is a longing inside of him and he is eager to know more.

The ninth chapter is Raajavidyaa Raajaguhya Yoga, the path of royal knowledge, kingly knowledge and royal secrets. This is the knowledge of true character, love, and dedication; the knowledge of surrender; the knowledge of the splendour of the most beautiful One, Supreme above all deities. Krishna makes it clear that the bhakta who surrenders to Him enjoys true intimacy with Him above all others. But this knowledge is a secret which is not given to everyone.

The tenth chapter is Vibhuti Yoga, the Divine Glory, where the Lord reveals to Arjuna His two aspects: sagun Brahman and nirgun Brahman. Paramahamsa Vishwananda explains in his commentary:

"Lord Krishna reveals that He is in everything, and it is only Him who manifests in different aspects and plays different roles. He manifests into a flower and He plays the role of the flower. He manifests into each one of you. Each person is actually His own Divine manifestation, yet, even if He manifests through all, He's still the Supreme in everything. He's not bound by limitation, whereas the individual soul is bound by limitation, by Maya, until it becomes fully God-realised. Then, upon reaching God-Realisation, the ego self becomes completely dissolved in the Ultimate, and that's where Narayana Krishna, the Ultimate One, is revealed."

Paramahamsa Vishwananda outlines the next few chapters of the *Gita* like this:

"In the last verse of Chapter 10, Bhagavan says to Arjuna, 'I have told you everything about My glory, I have expressed to you where, and in which form, My glories are present'. But Bhagavan then says, 'Okay, you've heard all this, but of what use is it? This knowledge is too much for you, my dear Arjuna. You are not a Jyaana yogi. You are a bhakta and a bhakta doesn't need to bother too much about this. Why fill your mind? Why drive yourself crazy?' Bhagavan says to him in a former verse, 'Surrender to Me! Find Me everywhere. With whatever you do, bear in mind that it is for Me that you are doing it. [...] For what use have I told you all this? For your mind, - if you look at it with your mind - you have heard my great wonders; they have purified you.' So, in this chapter here, Bhagavan reveals Himself to Arjuna, not just in words, because Arjuna has made himself ready. There is not a trace of doubt inside of him, so the Lord can reveal Himself in His cosmic Form.

"The eleventh chapter, Vishwarupa Darshana Yoga, is about the supreme vision of the universal cosmic form of the Lord. [...] Know one thing, for the bhaktas who are fully surrendered, the Lord reveals His cosmic Form in the core of themselves. And sometimes, due to the love of a bhakta, He also takes the form outside."

"...The twelfth chapter is Bhakti Yoga, where Bhagavan Himself explains about Bhakti, how one can attain surrender - not a vision of Him. Don't ask for a vision. Attain surrender. [...] if one makes an effort to change, opening the heart, opening the mind, then one receives Grace. And it is Grace; it's not your effort. You appear to do it, but after Realisation you realise that it's only the Lord Himself who is doing it. It is the cosmic energy that flows. What can you do? Nothing. If the Lord doesn't wish you to breathe, you can't even breathe. [...] This is one of the shortest chapters. It's funny that about Bhakti, which is the ultimate, the most important type of yoga, Bhagavan doesn't need to say much, because in Bhakti there's not much to say - all count on Grace only."

The thirteenth chapter is Kshetrakshetrajna Vibhaaga Yoga. In this chapter, Krishna begins to introduce new topics of discussion, the most prominent of which is the difference between Prakriti (Kshetra; nature) and Purusha (Kshetrajna; Self). Arjuna wishes to further understand his own nature and where he stands in relation to God and His creation. What is the body? What is the soul? These are the principle questions of the Sankhya philosophy, the process of identifying and distinguishing between the soul and material matter.

The fourteenth chapter is Gunatraya Vibhaaga Yoga. Paramahamsa Vishwananda explains:

"In this chapter we will see how Bhagavan Krishna differentiates the three gunas: rajas, sattva and tamas. All is God, yes. But He explains to Arjuna how important are the good qualities in a bhakta. Without good qualities one can't advance. He will speak of the effect of good qualities, and how they are beneficial for the bhakta to advance. [...] He also explains how, through the tamasic guna, one is thrown into the cycle of birth and death and gets hanged; how, through the rajas guna, one goes through life performing one's own actions; and how, through sattvic guna, one becomes liberated or frees oneself. And not only the three gunas, but also how to rise above the three gunas - how to excel, and not trap oneself in this drama of the outside reality. To attain God-Realisation, you have to rise above the three gunas."

At the end of this chapter, Lord Krishna reminds Arjuna that the best way to attain spiritual perfection is through the means of Bhakti. Although the result of transcending the gunas and obtaining knowledge of the Self can be reached through other methods, Bhakti is emphasised by the Lord as the ideal path.

The fifteenth chapter is Purushottama Yoga. In this chapter Bhagavan is introducing Ishvara, the Purushottama who is beyond Prakriti and the Purusha. The Supreme Deity, which Krishna identifies as Himself, lies beyond even the Self and is the origin of all things. This chapter speaks of the unity that can be attained with this Supreme Lord.

The sixteenth chapter is Daivaasurasampad Vibhaaga Yoga. As Paramahamsa Vishwananda describes it:

"This chapter is about the discrimination between good qualities and negative qualities. Here I am using the word discrimination. Discrimination is not judging. True discrimination helps you discriminate between good and bad, yet you are above good and bad. [...] Bhagavan Krishna explains to Arjuna how one recognises somebody who is God-realised, who has divine qualities and how one recognises those who have demonic qualities, evil qualities inside of them. Here it's not about looking at somebody else, but inside oneself."

The seventeenth chapter, Shraddhaatraya Vibhaaga Yoga, is about the three types of faith and the distinction between them. In this chapter, Lord Krishna touches upon several different themes, focusing mainly on the analysis of different aspects of life which are governed and affected by the three gunas (sattva, rajas, and tamas): what one eats, how one speaks, and one's actions, including religious acts, sacrifices, austerities and charity. In the final verses, Bhagavan Krishna explains the deep meaning of the mantra *Om Tat Sat*.

Paramahamsa Vishwananda explains, "The *Gita* is about how to love God and let go of the negative qualities. All these qualities, which Bhagavan Krishna talks about in this chapter, are not outside; you are born with them. Some of the qualities are stronger than the others, but nevertheless if you are not aware, if you are not attentive, conscious about them; then you let yourself be overruled by these qualities. The best of all qualities is the Love that Bhagavan has put inside your heart and that's true Love. [...] Here Bhagavan Krishna has given this knowledge saying, 'There are the three gunas: tamasic, rajasic and sattvic.' [...] This is just to show you how to distinguish these qualities. But beyond that, in Chapter 9, verse 9, Bhagavan Krishna says, 'Nor do these works bind me, O Dhananjaya, for I am seated above as if indifferent, unattached to those actions.' And that's what we have to focus on, not on the qualities. We need to transcend these qualities, but once we have transcended them, we have to reach Him only."

Then, the eighteenth chapter is Moksha Sannyasa Yoga. In this final Chapter of the *Gita*, Arjuna asks his final questions to Krishna. They all point in one direction - clarifying the route to Moksha, total Realisation. After discussing many topics, Krishna gives particular emphasis to three paths leading to Moksha: Karma Yoga, Jyaana Yoga and most importantly and most emphasised by Bhagavan, Bhakti Yoga. Krishna then concludes his own teachings and summarises them for Arjuna, giving specific instructions in relation to what He wishes his disciple to do with the teachings he has received.

Paramahamsa Vishwananda summarises it by saying: "In this chapter, Bhagavan speaks about Moksha Sannyasa Yoga, the path of complete surrender; the path of attaining the Lord; the path of letting go of the outside completely to attain His Grace. The path of removing all the barriers which separate the Lord and the bhakta - the lover and the Beloved - and attaining this supreme bliss, which we call God-Realisation. He explains that whatever you do, if it is with an attitude of surrender, wherever you are, the Lord is not far away from you, He is seated inside your heart. When you perform your duty, with full love, when you love what the Lord has given you, you become free. Then Bhagavan Himself will reveal Himself wherever you are."

He adds: "This knowledge of the *Gita* destroys sins and renders salvation, not only to the person who is hearing or reading it, but to the whole of humanity. One who with calm mind, studies and listens to one or one half of a chapter, or a quarter of a chapter, or a part of these slokas, is entitled to receive salvation. [...] This is the punya one receives: just by listening to, or by reading the *Gita*, one is freed and becomes a source of liberation for others. [...] Whoever meditates upon the *Gita*, reading it daily and trying to understand the verses, will be overwhelmed with Love. The daily reciting of one verse, and also trying to know the meaning, will imbue one with Love and spirit. And when this happens, one will be fully transformed into the Divine Self. Lord Krishna Himself says, 'This is My conviction, this is My assurance, My promise.' Whoever studies the *Gita* wholeheartedly will come to Him. Whoever seeks Him, He will reveal Himself to them."

With that in mind, there is truly nothing more that can be said as introduction.

We hope you enjoy your journey through the extraordinary pages of the *Shreemad Bhagavad Gita*, and that you arrive at your destination, the Feet of the Lord within your heart, transformed by His Grace.

- Bhakti Marga Publications

MAHABHARAT FAMILY TREE: SIMPLIFIED

COLOUR-CODED SYMBOLS

■	main male	□	relevant female
▣	main female	□□	gender change
□	deva	⌐ ¬ (dashed)	**Krishna's family** (partial view)
□	relevant male	¦ ¦ (dash-dot)	**Draupadi's family**

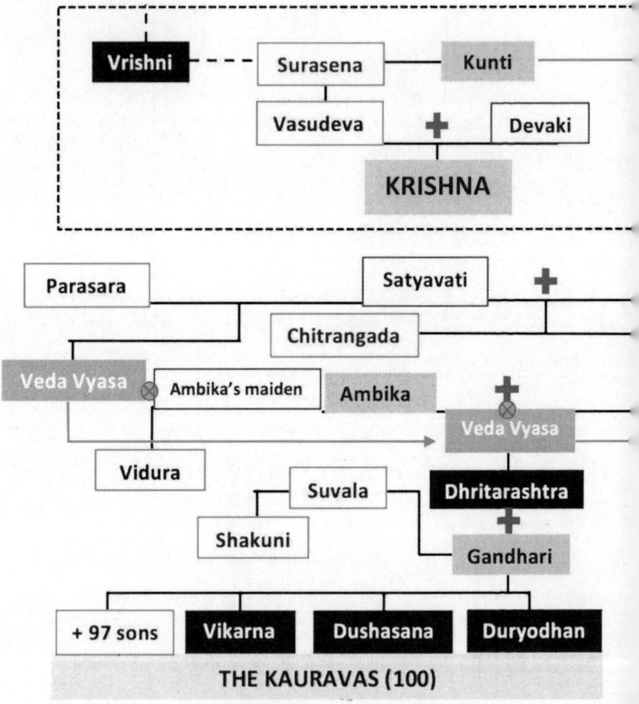

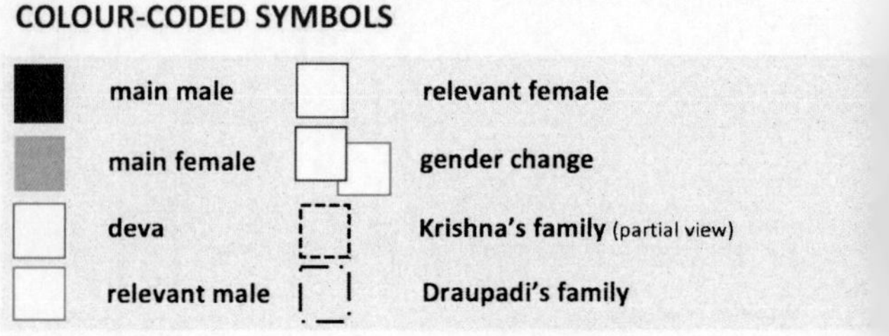

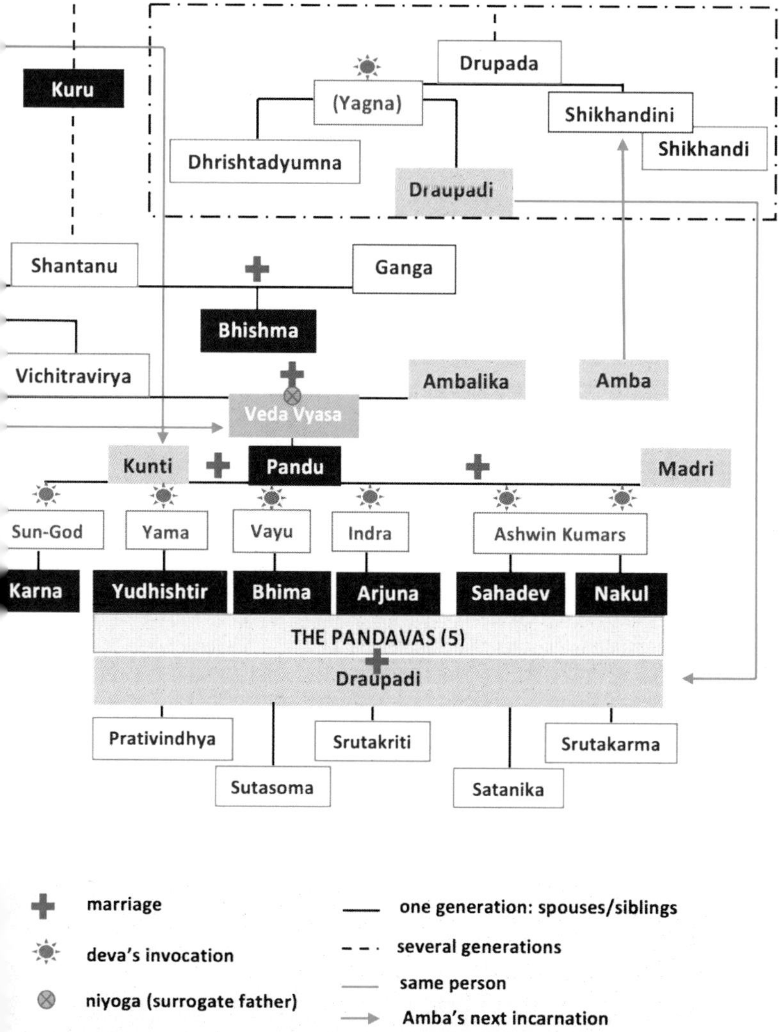

Drupada
(Yagna)
Shikhandini
Shikhandi
Dhrishtadyumna
Draupadi
Kuru
Shantanu
Ganga
Bhishma
Vichitravirya
Ambalika
Amba
Veda Vyasa
Kunti
Pandu
Madri
Sun-God
Yama
Vayu
Indra
Ashwin Kumars
Karna
Yudhishtir
Bhima
Arjuna
Sahadev
Nakul
THE PANDAVAS (5)
Draupadi
Prativindhya
Sutasoma
Srutakriti
Satanika
Srutakarma
marriage
deva's invocation
niyoga (surrogate father)
one generation: spouses/siblings
several generations
same person
Amba's next incarnation

CHAPTER 1
ARJUNA VISHAADA YOGA

atha prathamo 'dhyāyaḥ

Here begins the first chapter

Chapter 1, Verse 1

dhṛtarāṣṭra uvāca
dharmakṣetre kurukṣetre
samavetā yuyutsavaḥ
māmakāḥ pāṇḍavāś caiva
kim akurvata sañjaya

Dhritarashtra asks: On the field of Kurukshetra, the field of the working out of the dharma, gathered together, eager for battle, what did they do, O Sanjaya, my people and the Pandavas?

Chapter 1, Verse 2

sañjaya uvāca
dṛṣṭva tu pāṇḍavānīkaṁ
vyūḍhaṁ duryodhanas tadā
ācāryam upasaṅgamya
rājā vacanam abravīt

Sanjaya says: Then the prince, Duryodhan, having seen the army of the Pandavas arrayed in battle order, approaches his teacher, Dronacharya, and speaks these words:

Chapter 1, Verse 3

paśyaitām pāṇḍu-putrāṇām
ācārya mahatīṁ camūm
vyūḍhāṁ drupada-putreṇa
tava śiṣyeṇa dhīmatā

"Behold this mighty host of the sons of Pandu, O Acharya, arrayed by Drupada's son, your intelligent disciple."

Chapter 1, Verses 4-6

atra śūrā maheṣvās
bhīmārjuna samā yudhi
yuyodhāno virāṭaśca
drupadaśca mahārathaḥ

dhṛṣṭaketuś-cekitānaḥ
kāśi-rājaśca vīryavān
purujit-kunti-bhojaśca
śaibyaśca nara-puṅgavaḥ

yudhāmanyuśca vikrānta
uttamaujāśca vīryavān
saubhadro draupadeyāśca
sarva eva mahārathāḥ

"Here in this mighty army are heroes and great bowmen who are equal in battle to Bhima and Arjuna: Yuyudhana, Virat and Drupada of the great chariot, Dhrishtaketu, Chekitana and the valiant prince of Kashi, Purujit and Kuntibhoja, and Shaibya, foremost among men. Yudhamanyu, the strong, and Uttamauja, the victorious; Subhadra's son (Abhimanyu), and the sons of Draupadi; all of them of great prowess."

Chapter 1, Verse 7

asmākaṁ tu viśiṣṭā ye
tān-nibodha dvijottama
nāyakāḥ mama sainyasya
saṁjñārthaṁ tān bravīmi te

"On our side also, know those who are the most distinguished. O best of the twice-born, the leaders of my army; these I name to you for your special notice."

Chapter 1, Verses 8-9

bhavān bhīṣmaśca karnaśca
kṛpaśca samitiñjayaḥ
aśvatthāmā vikarṇaśca
saumadattas tathaiva ca

anye ca bahavaḥ śūrā
madārthe tyakta-jīvitāḥ
nānā-śāstra praharaṇāḥ
sarve yuddha-viśāradāḥ

"Yourself, Bhishma and Karna and Kripacharya, the victorious in battle, Ashvatthama, Vikarna, and Saumadatti also; and many other heroes have renounced their life for my sake, they are all armed with diverse weapons and missiles and all well-skilled in war."

Chapter 1, Verse 10

aparyāptaṁ tad asmakaṁ
balaṁ bhīṣmābhirakṣita
paryāptaṁ tvidam eteṣāṁ
balaṁ bhīmābhirakṣitam

"Unlimited is this army of ours and it is marshalled by Bhishma, while the army of theirs is limited, and they depend on Bhima."

Chapter 1, Verse 11

ayaneṣu ca sarveṣu
yathā-bhāgam avasthitāḥ
bhīṣmam evābhi-rakṣantu
bhavantaḥ sarva eva hi

"Therefore, all of you standing in your respective divisions in the different fronts of the battle, guard Bhishma."

Chapter 1, Verse 12

tasya sañjanayan harṣaṁ
kuru-vṛddhaḥ pitāmahaḥ
siṁhanādaṁ vinadyoccaiḥ
śaṅkhaṁ dadhmau pratāpavān

To cheer the heart of Duryodhan, the mighty grandsire (Bhishma), the Ancient of the Kurus, resounding the battlefield with a lion's roar, blows his conch.

Chapter 1, Verse 13

tataḥ śaṅkhāśca bheryaśca
paṇavānaka-gomukhāḥ
sahasaivābhyahanyanta
sa śabdas-tumulo'bhavat

Then conches and kettledrums, tabors and drums and horns, suddenly blared forth, and the clamour becomes tremendous.

Chapter 1, Verse 14

tataḥ śvetair-hayair-yukte
mahati syandane sthitau
mādhavaḥ pāṇḍavaś caiva
divyau śaṅkhau pradadhmatuḥ

Then, seated in their great chariot, harnessed to white horses, Madhava (Sri Krishna) and the son of Pandu (Arjuna) blow their divine conches.

Chapter 1, Verses 15-16

pāñcajanyaṁ hṛṣīkeśo
devadattaṁ dhanañjayaḥ
pauṇḍraṁ dadhmau mahā-śaṅkhaṁ
bhīma-karmā vṛkodaraḥ
anantavijayaṁ rājā
kuntī-putro yudhiṣṭhiraḥ
nakulaḥ sahadevaśca
sughoṣa maṇi-puṣpakau

Sri Krishna blows his conch, Panchajanya, Arjuna blows his, named Devadatta, and Bhima of terrible deeds, blows the great conch, Paundra. King Yudhishtir, the son of Kunti, blows his conch Ananta-vijaya, and Nakul and Sahadev blow their conches, Sughosha and Mani-pushpaka.

Chapter 1, Verses 17-18

kāśyaśca parameṣ-vasaḥ
śikhaṇḍī ca mahārathaḥ
dhṛṣṭadyumno virāṭaśca
sātyakiś-cāparājitaḥ

drupado draupadeyāśca
sarvaśaḥ pṛthivī-pate
saubhadraśca mahā-bāhuḥ
śaṅkhān dadhmuḥ pṛthak pṛthak

And the King of Kashi; the supreme archer, Shikhandi the mighty warrior, Dhrishtadyumna and Virat; Satyaki the invincible; Drupada and the sons of Draupadi, and the strong-armed son of Subhadra - all, O king, blow their various conches again and again.

Chapter 1, Verse 19

sa ghoṣo dhārtarāṣṭrāṇāṁ
hṛdayāni vyadārayat
nabhaśca pṛthivīṁ caiva
tumulo'bhyanunādayan

That tumultuous uproar, resounding through earth and sky, tears the hearts of the sons of Dhritarashtra.

Chapter 1, Verse 20

atha vyavasthitān dṛṣṭvā
dhārtarāṣṭrān kapi-dhvajaḥ
pravṛtte śastra-sampāte
dhanur udyamya pāṇḍavaḥ
hṛṣīkeśaṁ tadā vākyam
idam āha mahī-pate

Then, beholding the sons of Dhritarashtra standing in battle order, and the flight of missiles ready to begin, the son of Pandu (Arjuna), whose emblem is an ape, takes up his bow and speaks these words to Sri Krishna, O king:

Chapter 1, Verses 21-23

arjuna uvāca
senayor-ubhayor madhye
rathaṁ sthāpaya me'cyuta

yāvad etān nirīkṣe'haṁ
yoddhu-kāmān avasthitān
kair-mayā saha yoddhavyam
asmin raṇa-samudyame

yotsyamānān avekṣehaṁ
ya ete'tra samāgatāḥ
dhārtarāṣṭrasya durbuddher
yuddhe priya cikīrṣavaḥ

Arjuna says: O Achyuta (the faultless, the immovable), station my chariot between these two armies, so that I may view these myriads standing, longing for battle. I wish to see who I am to fight, and look upon those who have come here to champion the cause of the evil-minded son of Dhritarashtra.

Chapter 1, Verses 24-25

sañjaya uvāca
evam ukto hṛṣīkeśo
guḍākeśena bhārata
senayor-ubhayor madhye
sthāpayitvā rathottamam

bhiṣma droṇa pramukhataḥ
sarveṣāṁ ca mahīkṣitām
uvāca pārtha paśyaitān
samavetān kurūn iti

Sanjaya says: Thus addressed by Gudakesha (one who has overcome sleep: Arjuna), Sri Krishna, O Bharata, having stationed the best of all chariots between the two armies, in front of Bhishma, Drona and all the princes of this Earth, says, "O Paartha (Arjuna), behold these Kurus gathered together."

Chapter 1, Verse 26

tatrāpaśyat sthitān pārthaḥ
pitṝn atha pita-mahān
ācāryān mātulān bhrātṝn
putrān pautrān sakhīṁs tathā
śvaśurān suhṛdaścaiva
senayor-ubhayor api

Then Arjuna sees standing on opposite sides, uncles and grandsires, teachers, brothers, cousins, sons and grandsons, comrades, fathers-in-law, and benefactors.

Chapter 1, Verse 27

tān samīkṣya sa kaunteyaḥ
sarvān bandhūn avasthitān
kṛpayā parayāviṣṭo
viṣīdann idam abravīt

Seeing all these kinsmen standing thus arrayed, Kaunteya (Arjuna), invaded by great pity, utters this in sadness and dejection:

Chapter 1, Verses 28-30

arjuna uvāca
dṛṣṭvemaṁ svajanaṁ kṛṣṇa
yuyutsaṁ samupasthitam

sīdanti mama gātrāṇi
mukhaṁ ca pariśuṣyati
vepathuśca śarīre me
roma harṣaśca jāyate

gāṇḍīvaṁ sramsate hastāt
tvak caiva pari-dahyate
na ca śaknomy-avasthātuṁ
bhramatīva ca me manaḥ

Arjuna says: Seeing my own people, O Krishna, arrayed for battle, my limbs collapse and my mouth is parched, my body shakes and my hair stands on end; Gandiva (Arjuna's bow) slips from my hand, and all my skin seems to be burning.

Chapter 1, Verse 31

nimittāni ca paśyāmi
viparītāni keśava
na ca śreyo'nupaśyāmi
hatvā svajanam āhave

I am not able to stand and my mind seems to be whirling; also I see evil omens, O Keshava.

Chapter 1, Verse 32

na kāṅkṣe vijayaṁ kṛṣṇa
na ca rājyaṁ sukhāni ca
kiṁ no rājyena govinda
kiṁ bhogair jīvitena vā

Nor do I see any good in slaying my own people in battle. O Krishna, I desire not victory, nor kingdoms, nor pleasures.

Chapter 1, Verses 33-36

yeṣām arthe kāṅkṣitaṁ no
rājyaṁ bhogāḥ sukhāni ca
ta ime' vasthitā yuddhe
prāṇāṁs tyaktvā dhanāni ca

ācāryāḥ pitaraḥ putrāṁs
tathaiva ca pitāmahāḥ
mātulāḥ śvaśurāḥ pautrāḥ
śyālāḥ sambandhinas tathā

etān na hantum icchāmi
ghnato'pi madhusūdana
api trailokya rājyasya
hetoḥ kiṁ nu mahīkṛte

nihatya dhārtarāṣṭrān naḥ
kiṁ prītiḥ syāj-janārdana
pāpam evāśrayed asmān
hatvaitān ātatāyinaḥ

What is a kingdom to us, O Govinda, what enjoyment, what is even life? Those for whose sake we desire a kingdom, enjoyments and pleasures, they stand here in battle, abandoning life and riches - teachers, fathers, sons, as well as grandsires, brothers, fathers-in-law, grandsons, brothers-in-law, and others of kin; these I would not consent to slay, though myself slain, O Madhusudana, even for the kingdom of the three worlds, how then for Earth? What pleasures can be ours after killing the sons of Dhritarashtra, O Janardana?

Chapter 1, Verse 37

tasmān nārhā vayaṁ hantuṁ
dhārtarāṣṭrān svabandhavān
svajanaṁ hi kathaṁ hatvā
sukhinaḥ syāma mādhava

Sin will take hold of us in slaying them, though they are the aggressors. So it is not fit that we kill the sons of Dhritarashtra, our kinsmen; indeed how may we be happy, O Madhava, killing our own people?

Chapter 1, Verses 38-39

yady-apyete na paśyanti
lobhopahata cetasaḥ
kula-kṣaya-kṛtaṁ doṣaṁ
mitra-drohe ca pātakam

kathaṁ na jñeyam asmābhiḥ
pāpād asmān nivartitum
kula-kṣaya-kṛtaṁ doṣaṁ
prapaśyadbhir janārdana

Although these, with a consciousness clouded with greed, see no guilt in the destruction of the family, no crime in hostility to friends, why should we not have the wisdom to recoil from such a sin, O Janardana, we who see the evil in the destruction of the family?

Chapter 1, Verse 40

kula-kṣaye praṇaśyanti
kula-dharmāḥ sanātanāḥ
dharme naṣṭe kulaṁ kṛtsnam
adharmo'bhibhavaty-uta

In the annihilation of the family, the eternal traditions of the family are destroyed; in the collapse of traditions, lawlessness overcomes the whole family.

Chapter 1, Verse 41

adharmābhi-bhavāt kṛṣṇa
praduṣyanti kula-striyaḥ
strīṣu duṣṭāsu vārṣṇeya
jāyate varṇa-saṅkaraḥ

Owing to the predominance of lawlessness, O Krishna, the women of the family become corrupt; women corrupted lead to the confusion of the varnas (castes).

Chapter 1, Verse 42

saṅkaro narakāyaiva
kula-ghnānāṁ kulasya ca
patanti pitaro hyeṣāṁ
lupta-piṇḍodaka-kriyāḥ

This confusion leads the family and the destroyers of the family to Hell; for their ancestors fall, deprived of pinda (rice offering) and libations.

Chapter 1, Verse 43

doṣair etaiḥ kula-ghnānāṁ
varṇa-saṅkara-kārakaiḥ
utsādyante jāti-dharmāḥ
kula-dharmāśca śāśvatāḥ

By these misdeeds of the destroyers of the family, leading to the confusion of the castes, the eternal laws of the clan and moral law of the family will be destroyed.

Chapter 1, Verse 44

utsanna-kula-dharmāṇāṁ
manuṣyāṇāṁ janārdana
narake'niyataṁ vāso
bhavatīty-anuśuśruma

And men whose family morals are corrupted, live forever in Hell. Thus have we heard.

Chapter 1, Verse 45

aho bata mahat pāpaṁ
kartuṁ vyavasitā vayam
yad rājya sukha lobhena
hantuṁ sva-janam udyatāḥ

Alas! We were engaged in committing a great sin, we who were endeavouring to kill our own people through greed for the pleasures of kingship.

Chapter 1, Verse 46

yadi mām apratīkāram
aśastraṁ śastra-pāṇayaḥ
dhārtarāṣṭrā raṇe hanyus
tan-me kṣemataraṁ bhavet

It would be better for me that the sons of Dhritarashtra, armed as they are, should slay me as I am, unarmed and unresisting.

Chapter 1, Verse 47

sañjaya uvāca
evam uktvā'rjunaḥ saṅkhye
rathopastha upāviśat
visṛjya saśaraṁ cāpaṁ
śoka saṁvigna mānasaḥ

Sanjaya says: Having thus spoken on the battlefield, Arjuna sinks down on the seat of the chariot, casting down the divine bow, his spirit overwhelmed with sorrow.

hariḥ oṁ tat sat
iti śrīmad bhagavad gītā sūpaniṣatsu
brahmavidyāyāṁ yoga śāstre śrī kṛṣṇārjuna
saṁvāde arjuna viṣāda yogaḥ nāma
prathamo 'dhyāyaḥ

Thus ends Chapter 1: Arjuna Vishaada Yoga, from the dialogue between Sri Krishna and Arjuna in the *Upanishad* known as *Shreemad Bhagavad Gita*, the science of the Absolute, the yoga shastra.

CHAPTER 2
SANKHYA YOGA

atha dvitīyo 'dhyāyaḥ

Here begins the second chapter

Chapter 2, Verse 1

sañjaya uvāca
taṁ tathā kṛpayāviṣṭaṁ
aśā-pūrṇā-kulekṣaṇam
viṣīdantam idaṁ vākyam
uvāca madhusūdanaḥ

Sanjaya says: To him thus invaded by pity, his eyes full and distressed with tears, his heart overcome by depression and discouragement, Krishna speaks these words.

Chapter 2, Verse 2

śrī bhagavān uvāca
kutas tvā kaśmalam idaṁ
viṣame samupasthitam
anāryājuṣṭam asvargyam
akīrtikaram arjuna

The Lord says: When did this dejection come to you, this stain and darkness of the soul, in the hour of difficulty and peril, O Arjuna? This is not the way cherished by the noble man: this mood came not from Heaven, nor can it lead to Heaven, and on Earth it is the forfeiting of glory.

Chapter 2, Verse 3

klaibyaṁ mā sma gamaḥ pārtha
naitat-tvayyupapadyate
kṣudraṁ hṛdaya daurbalyaṁ
tyaktvottiṣṭha parantapa

Fall not from the virility of a fighter and a hero, O Paartha! It does not befit you. Shake off this paltry faint-heartedness and arise, O scourge of your enemy!

Chapter 2, Verse 4

arjuna uvāca
kathaṁ bhīṣmam ahaṁ saṅkhye
droṇaṁ ca madhusūdana
iṣubhiḥ pratiyotsyāmi
pūjārhāv-arisūdana

Arjuna says: How, O Madhusudana, shall I strike Bhishma and Drona with weapons in battle, they who are worthy of worship?

Chapter 2, Verse 5

gurūn ahatvā hi mahānubhāvān
śreyo bhoktuṁ bhaikṣyam apīha loke
hatvārtha kāmāṁs tu gurūn ihaiva
bhuñjīya bhogān rudhira-pradigdhān

It is better to live in this world even on alms than to slay these high-souled gurus. Slaying these gurus, I would only taste blood-stained enjoyments in this world.

Chapter 2, Verse 6

na caitad vidmaḥ kataran no garīyo
yadvā jayema yadi vā no jayeyuḥ
yān eva hatvā na jijīviṣāmas
te'vasthitāḥ pramukhe dhārtarāṣṭhrāḥ

Nor do I know which is better for us, that we should conquer them or they conquer us. Before us stand the sons of Dhritarashtra, who if we slay, we would lose all desire to live.

Chapter 2, Verse 7

kārpaṇya doṣopahata svabhāvaḥ
pṛcchāmi tvāṁ dharma samūḍha cetāḥ
yacchreyaḥ syān niścitaṁ brūhi tan me
śiṣyas te śādhi māṁ tvāṁ prapannam

It is poorness of spirit that has smitten away from me, my (true heroic) nature; my deluded mind is bewildered in its view of right and wrong. I ask You which may be the better - tell me decisively. I take refuge in You as a disciple. Enlighten me.

Chapter 2, Verse 8

na hi prapaśyāmi mamāpanudyād
yacchokam ucchoṣaṇam indriyāṇām
avāpya bhūmāv-asapatnam-ṛddham
rājyaṁ suraṇām api cādhipatyam

Even if I should attain rich and unrivalled kingdoms on Earth or even the sovereignty of the gods, it would not take from me this sorrow that dries up my senses.

Chapter 2, Verse 9

sañjaya uvāca
evam uktvā hṛṣīkeśaṁ
guḍakeśaḥ parantapa
na yotsya iti govindam
uktvā tūṣṇīṁ babhūva ha

Sanjaya says: Gudakesha (Arjuna), terror of his foes, having thus spoken to Krishna, then says to Krishna, "I will not fight!" and becomes silent.

Chapter 2, Verse 10

tam uvāca hṛṣikeśaḥ
prahasann iva bhārata
senayor ubhayor madhye
viṣīdantaṁ idaṁ vacaḥ

To him thus depressed and discouraged, Krishna, smiling, O king, speaks these words between the two armies.

Chapter 2, Verse 11

śrī bhagavān uvāca
aśocyān anvaśocas tvaṁ
prajñāvādāṁśca bhāṣase
gatāsūn agatāsūṁśca
nānuśocanti paṇḍitāḥ

The Lord says: You grieve for those who should not be grieved for, yet you speak words of wisdom. The enlightened man does not mourn for either the living or for the dead.

Chapter 2, Verse 12

na tvevāhaṁ jātu nāsaṁ
na tvaṁ neme janādhipāḥ
na caiva na bhaviṣyāmaḥ
sarve vayamataḥ param

There was never a time that I did not exist, nor you, Arjuna, nor these kings of men; nor is it true that any of us shall ever cease to exist hereafter.

Chapter 2, Verse 13

dehino'smin yathā dehe
kaumāraṁ yauvanaṁ jarā
tathā dehāntara prāptir
dhīras tatra na muhyati

As the soul passes physically through childhood, youth and old age, so it passes on to the changing of the body. The self-composed man does not allow himself to be disturbed or blinded by this.

Chapter 2, Verse 14

mātrā sparśās tu kaunteya
śītoṣṇa sukha-duḥkhadāḥ
āgamāpāyino'nityās
tāṁs titikṣasva bhārata

The interaction of senses and objects, O son of Kunti, give cold and heat, pleasure and pain, transient things which come and go. Endure them, O Arjuna.

Chapter 2, Verse 15

yaṁ hi na vyathayantyete
puruṣaṁ puruṣarṣabha
sama duḥkha sukhaṁ dhīraṁ
so'mṛtatvāya kalpate

The man who these do not trouble or pain, O lion-hearted among men, the firm and wise who is equal in pleasure and suffering, makes himself apt for immortality.

Chapter 2, Verse 16

nāsato vidyate bhāvo
nābhāvo vidyate sataḥ
ubhayor api dṛṣṭo'ntas
tvanayos tattva darśibhiḥ

That which really is, cannot go out of existence, just as that which is non-existent cannot come into being. The end of this opposition of 'is' and 'is not' has been perceived by the seers of essential truths.

Chapter 2, Verse 17

avināśi tu tad viddhi
yena sarvam idaṁ tatam
vināśam avyayasyāsya
na kaścit kartum arhati

Know that to be imperishable from which all this is extended. Who can slay the immortal spirit?

Chapter 2, Verse 18

antavanta ime dehā
nityasy-oktāḥ śarīriṇaḥ
anāśino'prameyasya
tasmāt yuddhyasva bhārata

Finite bodies have an end, but that which possesses and uses the body is infinite, illimitable, eternal, indestructible. Therefore, fight, O Bharata (Arjuna).

Chapter 2, Verse 19

ya enaṁ vetti hantāraṁ
yaś cainaṁ manyate hatam
ubhau tau na vijānīto
nāyaṁ hanti na hanyate

He who regards this (the soul) as a slayer, and he who thinks it is slain, both of them fail to perceive the truth. The soul does not slay, nor is it slain.

Chapter 2, Verse 20

na jāyate mriyate vā kadācin
nāyaṁ bhūtvā bhavitā vā na bhūyaḥ
ajo nityaḥ śāśvato 'yaṁ purāṇo
na hanyate hanyamāne śarīre

This is not born, nor does it die, nor is it a thing that comes into being once and passing away will never come into being again. It is unborn, ancient, everlasting; it is not slain with the slaying of the body.

Chapter 2, Verse 21

vedāvināśinaṁ nityaṁ
ya enam ajam avyayam
kathaṁ sa puruṣaḥ pārtha
kaṁ ghātayati hanti kam

Who knows it as immortal, eternal, imperishable, spiritual existence, how can that man slay, O Paartha, or cause to be slain?

Chapter 2, Verse 22

vāsānsi jīrṇāni yathā vihāya
navāni gṛhṇāti naro'parāṇi
tathā śarīrāṇi vihāya jīrṇāny
anyāni sanyāti navāni dehī

The embodied soul casts away old bodies and takes up new bodies, as a man changes worn-out clothes for new.

Chapter 2, Verse 23

nainaṁ chindanti śastrāṇi
nainaṁ dahati pāvakaḥ
na cainaṁ kledayanty-āpo
na śoṣayati mārutaḥ

Weapons cannot cut it, nor the fire burn it, nor do the waters drench it, nor the wind dry it.

Chapter 2, Verse 24

acchedyo'yam adāhyo'yaṁ
akledyo'śoṣya eva ca
nityaḥ sarvagataḥ sthāṇur
acalo'yam sanātanaḥ

It cannot be cut, it is incombustible, it can neither be drenched nor dried. Eternally stable, immobile, all-pervading, ever-existing.

Chapter 2, Verse 25

avyakto'yam acintyo'yam
avikāryo'yam ucyate
tasmād evaṁ viditvainaṁ
nānuśocitum arhasi

It is unmanifest, it is unthinkable, it is immutable, so is it described; therefore, knowing it as such, you should not grieve.

Chapter 2, Verse 26

atha cainaṁ nitya jātam
nityaṁ vā manyase mṛtam
tathāpi tvaṁ mahābāho
naivaṁ śocitum arhasi

Even if you think of the Self as being constantly subject to birth and death, still, O mighty-armed, you should not grieve.

Chapter 2, Verse 27

jātasya hi dhruvo mṛtyur
dhruvaṁ janma mṛtasya ca
tasmād aparihārye 'rthe
na tvaṁ śocitum arhasi

Death is certain for those who are born, and birth is certain for those who die; therefore what is inevitable ought not to be a cause of your sorrow.

Chapter 2, Verse 28

avyaktādīni bhūtāni
vyakta-madhyāni bhārata
avyakta nidhanānyeva
tatra kā parivedana

Beings are unmanifest in the beginning, manifest in the middle, unmanifest likewise are they in disintegration. What is there to be grieved at, O Bharata?

Chapter 2, Verse 29

āścaryavat paśyati kaścid enam
āścaryavad vadati tathaiva cānyaḥ
āścaryavac cainam anyaḥ śṛṇoti
śrutvāpy-enaṁ veda na caiva kaścit

One sees it as a mystery or one speaks of it or hears of it as a mystery, yet none truly know it. That Self, which we look on and speak of and hear of as that which is wonderful, beyond our comprehension, no human mind has ever known this Absolute.

Chapter 2, Verse 30

dehī nityam avadhyo'yaṁ
dehe sarvasya bhārata
tasmāt sarvāṇi bhūtāni
na tvaṁ śocitum arhasi

This dweller in the body of everyone is eternal and indestructible, O Bharata, therefore you should not grieve for any creature.

Chapter 2, Verse 31

sva-dharmam api cāvekṣya
na vikampitum arhasi
dharmyāddhi yuddhāc-chreyo
'nyat kṣatriyasya na vidyate

Looking to do your own duty, you should not tremble; there is no greater good for the Kshatriya than righteous battle.

Chapter 2, Verse 32

yadṛcchayā copapannaṁ
svarga dvāram apāvṛtam
sukhinaḥ kṣatriyāḥ pārtha
labhante yuddham īdṛśam

Happy are the Kshatriyas, O Arjuna, to whom a war such as this comes of its own accord; it opens the gates to Heaven.

Chapter 2, Verse 33

atha-cet tvam imaṁ dharmyaṁ
saṅgrāmaṁ na kariṣyasi
tataḥ sva-dharmaṁ kīrtiṁ ca
hitvā pāpam avāpsyasi

But if you do not fight this righteous battle, then you have abandoned your duty and virtue and your glory, and you shall incur only sin.

Chapter 2, Verse 34

akīrtiṁ cāpi bhūtāni
kathayiṣyanti te'vyayām
saṁbhāvitasya cākīrtir
maraṇād-atiricyate

Besides, men will recount your perpetual disgrace, and to an honourable man, dishonour is worse than death.

Chapter 2, Verse 35

bhayād raṇād uparataṁ
mansyante tvāṁ mahārathāḥ
yeṣāṁ ca tvaṁ bahu-mato
bhūtvā yāsyasi lāghavam

The mighty men will think you fled from the battle through fear, and you, whom all think highly of, will allow a stain to fall on your honour.

Chapter 2, Verse 36

avācya vādāṁśca bahūn
vadiṣyanti tavāhitāḥ
nindantas tava sāmarthyaṁ
tato duḥkhataraṁ nu kim

Many unseemly words will be spoken by your enemies, slandering your strength; what is worse grief than that?

Chapter 2, Verse 37

hato vā prāpsyasi svargaṁ
jitvā vā bhokṣyase mahīn
tasmād uttiṣṭha kaunteya
yuddhāya kṛta-niścayaḥ

If slain, you shall win Heaven, if victorious, you shall enjoy the Earth; therefore arise, O son of Kunti, and resolve to fight.

Chapter 2, Verse 38

sukha-duḥkhe same kṛtvā
lābhālābhau jayājayau
tato yuddhāya yujyasva
nainaṁ pāpam avāpsyasi

Make grief and happiness, loss and gain, victory and defeat equal to your soul and then turn to battle; this way you shall not incur sin.

Chapter 2, Verse 39

eṣā te'bhihitā sāṅkhye
buddhir yoge tvimāṁ śṛṇu
buddhyā-yukto yayā pārtha
karma-bandhaṁ prahāsyasi

O son of Pritha, this knowledge which has been taught to you so far concerns Sankhya. Hear now the teachings concerning yoga, for if you are in yoga, by this intelligence, you shall cast away the bondage of karma.

Chapter 2, Verse 40

nehābhikrama-nāśo'sti
pratyavāyo na vidyate
svalpam apyasya dharmasya
trāyate mahato bhayāt

On this path, no effort is lost, no obstacle prevails; even a little of this practice delivers one from great fear.

Chapter 2, Verse 41

vyavasāyātmikā buddhir
ekeha kuru-nandana
bahu-śākhā hyanantāśca
buddhayo'vyavasāyinām

In this practice, O Arjuna, the resolute mind is one-pointed; the thoughts of the irresolute are many-branched and endless.

Chapter 2, Verses 42-44

yām imāṁ puṣpitāṁ vācaṁ
pravadanty-avipaścitaḥ
veda-vāda-ratāḥ pārtha
nānyad astīti vādinaḥ

kāmātmānaḥ svarga-parā
janma-karma-phala-pradām
kriyā-viśeṣa bahulāṁ
bhogaiśvarya gatiṁ prati

bhogaiśvarya prasaktānāṁ
tayāpahṛta cetasām
vyavasāyātmikā buddhiḥ
samādhau na vidhīyate

Flowery speech, O Paartha is uttered by the unwise who rejoice in the words of the *Vedas*, declaring, "There is nothing superior to this!" They are full of desires and have Heaven as their goal. They teach rebirth as the result of actions and engage in various specific rites for the attainment of pleasure and power. Those who cling to pleasure and power are attracted by these teachings and are unable to develop the resolute will of a concentrated mind.

Chapter 2, Verse 45

trai-guṇya viṣayā vedā
nistrai-guṇyo bhavārjuna
nir-dvandvo nitya satvastho
nir-yoga kṣema ātmavān

The *Vedas* deal with the three gunas, O Arjuna. You must free yourself from the three gunas and from all duality. Abide in pure sattva; never care to acquire things or to protect what has been acquired; be established in the Self.

Chapter 2, Verse 46

yāvān artha udapāne
sarvataḥ saṁplutodake
tāvān sarveṣu vedeṣu
brāhmaṇasya vijānataḥ

As much use as there is in a well with water flooding on every side, so much is there in all the *Vedas* or the brahmin who has the knowledge of the Self.

Chapter 2, Verse 47 karmaṇy-evādhikāras te
mā phaleṣu kadācana
mā karma phala hetur bhūr
mā te saṅgo 'stv karmaṇi

You have the right to action, but only to action, never to its fruits; let not the fruits of your works be your motive, neither let there be in you any attachment to inactivity.

Chapter 2, Verse 48

yogasthaḥ kuru karmāṇi
saṅgaṁ tyaktvā dhanañjaya
siddhy-asiddhyoḥ samo bhūtvā
samatvaṁ yoga ucyate

Fixed in yoga do your actions, having abandoned attachment, having become equal in failure and success; for it is equality that is the essence of yoga.

Chapter 2, Verse 49

dūreṇa hyavaraṁ karma
buddhi-yogād dhanañjaya
buddhau śaraṇam anviccha
kṛpaṇāḥ phala-hetavaḥ

Works are far inferior to the yoga of the intelligence, O Dhananjaya. Rather, desire refuge in the intelligence; poor and wretched souls are they who make the fruit of their actions the object of their thoughts and activities.

Chapter 2, Verses 50-51

buddhi-yukto jahātīha
ubhe sukṛta duṣkṛte
tasmād yogāya yujyasva
yogaḥ karmasu kauśalam

karmajaṁ buddhi-yuktā hi
phalaṁ tyaktvā manīṣiṇaḥ
janma bandha vinirmuktāḥ
padaṁ gacchanty-anāmayam

Endowed with wisdom of equanimity, one discards here and now the fruits of good and evil deeds. Therefore, devote yourself to yoga. The performance of actions with a balanced mind is true yoga. The sages who have united their reason and will with the Divine, renounce the fruit which action yields and, liberated from the bondage of birth, they reach the status beyond misery.

Chapter 2, Verse 52

yadā te mohakalilaṁ
buddhir vyati-tariṣyati
tadā gantāsi nirvedaṁ
śrotavyasya śrutasya ca

When your intelligence crosses beyond the whirl of delusion, then you will become indifferent to scriptures already heard and to scriptures you are yet to hear.

Chapter 2, Verse 53

śruti vipratipannā te
yadā sthāsyasi niścalā
samādhāv-acalā buddhis
tadā yogam avāpsyasi

When your intellect, well-enlightened by listening to Me and firmly placed, remains unshaken in a concentrated mind, then you will attain the vision of the Self and attain yoga.

Chapter 2, Verse 54

arjuna uvāca
sthita-prajñāsya kā bhāṣā
samādhisthasya keśava
sthita-dhīḥ kiṁ prabhāṣata
kim āsīta vrajeta kim

Arjuna says: What is the mode of speech, O Krishna, of one of steady wisdom, who is established in the control of the mind? What does one of steady wisdom say? How does he sit? How does he move?

Chapter 2, Verse 55

śrī bhagavān uvāca
prajahāti yadā kāmān
sarvān pārtha manogatān
ātmany-evātmanā tuṣṭaḥ
sthita-prajñās tad-ocyate

The Lord says: When a man expels, O Paartha, all desires from the mind, and is satisfied in the Self by the Self, then is he considered stable in intelligence.

Chapter 2, Verse 56

duḥkheṣv-anudvigna-manāḥ
sukheṣu vigata spṛhaḥ
vīta-rāga bhaya krodhaḥ
sthita-dhīr munir ucyate

He whose mind is undisturbed in the midst of sorrows and pleasures is free from desire; he from whom liking, fear and wrath have passed away, is the sage of settled understanding.

Chapter 2, Verse 57

yaḥ sarvatrānabhisnehas
tat tat prāpya śubhāśubham
nābhinandati na dveṣṭi
tasya prajñā pratiṣṭhitā

He who has no attachment anywhere; he who, when encountering the agreeable or the disagreeable, feels neither attraction nor aversion - his wisdom is firmly established.

Chapter 2, Verse 58

yadā saṁharate cāyaṁ
kūrmo'ṅgānīva sarvaśaḥ
indriyāṇīndriyārthebhyas
tasya prajñā pratiṣṭhitā

He who withdraws his senses from the objects of sense, as the tortoise withdraws his limbs into his shell, his intelligence sits firmly founded in wisdom.

Chapter 2, Verse 59

viṣayā vinivartante
nirāhārasya dehinaḥ
rasa-varjaṁ raso'pyasya
paraṁ dṛṣṭvā nivartate

If one abstains from food, the objects of sense cease to affect one; but the taste for the sense objects remains. The taste also ceases when the Supreme is seen.

Chapter 2, Verse 60

yatato hyapi kaunteya
puruṣasya vipaścitaḥ
indriyāṇi pramāthīni
haranti prasabhaṁ manaḥ

Even the mind of the wise man who labours for perfection is carried away by the vehement insistence of the senses, O son of Kunti.

Chapter 2, Verse 61

tāni sarvāṇi saṁyamya
yukta āsīta matparaḥ
vaśe hi yasyendriyāṇi
tasya prajñā pratiṣṭhitā

Having brought all the senses under control, he must sit firmly in yoga, wholly given up to Me; he whose senses are mastered, his intelligence is firmly established (in its proper seat).

Chapter 2, Verse 62

dhyāyato viṣayān puṁsaḥ
saṅgas teṣūpajāyate
saṅgāt sañjāyate kāmaḥ
kāmāt krodho'bhijāyate

In him whose mind dwells on the objects of sense with absorbing interest, attachment to them is formed. From attachment arises desire. From desire, anger comes forth.

Chapter 2, Verse 63

krodhād-bhavati saṁmohaḥ
saṁmohāt smṛti-vibhramaḥ
smṛti-bhramśād buddhi-nāśo
buddhir-nāśāt praṇaśyati

Anger leads to bewilderment, from bewilderment comes loss of memory, and by that the intelligence is destroyed; from destruction of intelligence, one perishes.

Chapter 2, Verses 64-65

rāga-dveṣa viyuktais tu
viṣayān indriyaiś-caran
ātma-vaśyair vidheyātmā
prasādam adhigacchati

prasāde sarva-duḥkhānāṁ
hānir asyopajāyate
prasanna-cetaso hyāśu
buddhiḥ paryavatiṣṭhate

It is by moving among the sense-objects, but with the senses subjected to the Self, freed from liking and disliking, that one attains a large and sweet clearness of soul and temperament in which passion and grief find no place; the intelligence of such a man is rapidly established (in its proper seat).

Chapter 2, Verse 66

nāsti buddhir-ayuktasya
na cāpyuktasya bhāvanā
na cābhāvayataḥ śāntir
aśāntasya kutaḥ sukham

For one who is not in yoga, there is no intelligence, no concentration; for him without concentration, there is no peace; and for the restless, how can there be happiness?

Chapter 2, Verse 67

indriyāṇāṁ hi caratāṁ
yan mano'nuvidhīyate
tad asya harati prajñāṁ
vāyur nāvam ivāṁbhasi

When the mind follows the senses 'experiencing' their objects, the understanding is carried away by them, as the wind carries away a ship on the waters.

Chapter 2, Verse 68

tasmād yasya mahābāho
nigṛhītāni sarvaśaḥ
indriyāṇīndriyārthebhyas
tasya prajñā pratiṣṭhitā

Therefore, O mighty-armed, one who has utterly restrained the excitement of the senses by their objects, his intelligence sits firmly founded in calm Self-knowledge.

Chapter 2, Verse 69

yā niśā sarva bhūtānāṁ
tasyāṁ jāgarti saṁyamī
yasyāṁ jāgrati bhūtāni
sā niśā paśyato muneḥ

The self-controlled one is awake during what is night for all beings; when all beings are awake, that is the night to the enlightened one.

Chapter 2, Verse 70

apūryamāṇam acala pratiṣṭhaṁ
samudram āpaḥ praviśanti yadvat
tadvat kāmā yaṁ praviśanti sarve
sa śāntim āpnoti na kāmakāmī

One into whom all desires enter, as rivers enter the fullness of the ocean which remains undisturbed, attains peace, and not one who craves after objects of desire.

Chapter 2, Verse 71

vihāya kāmān yaḥ sarvān
pumāṁś-carati niḥspṛhaḥ
nirmamo nirahaṅkāraḥ
sa śāntim adhigacchati

He who abandons all desires and lives free from longing, who has no "I" or "mine", and has extinguished the sense of egoistic self-importance, attains peace.

Chapter 2, Verse 72

eṣā brāhmī-sthitiḥ pārtha
naināṁ prāpya vimuhyati
sthitvā'syām antakāle'pi
brahma-nirvāṇam ṛcchati

This is brahmi sthiti, O Arjuna. Having attained it, one is no longer bewildered; fixed in that state at the hour of death, one can attain the Brahman itself.

hariḥ oṁ tat sat
iti śrīmad bhagavad gītā sūpaniṣatsu
brahma vidyāyāṁ yoga śāstre śrī kṛṣṇārjuna
saṁvāde sāṅkhya yogaḥ nāma dvitīyo
'dhyāyaḥ

Thus ends Chapter 2: Sankhya Yoga, from the dialogue between Sri Krishna and Arjuna in the *Upanishad* known as *Shreemad Bhagavad Gita*, the science of the Absolute, the yoga shastra.

CHAPTER 3
KARMA YOGA

atha tṛtīyo 'dhyāyaḥ

Here begins the third chapter

Chapter 3, Verse 1

arjuna uvāca
jyāyasī cet karmaṇaste
matā buddhir-janārdana
tat kiṁ karmaṇi ghore māṁ
niyojayasi keśava

Arjuna says: If You hold intelligence (buddhi) to be greater than action (karma), O Krishna, why then do You, O Keshava, urge me to engage in this terrible deed?

Chapter 3, Verse 2

vyāmiśreṇaiva vākyena
buddhiṁ mohayasīva me
tad ekaṁ vada niścitya
yena śreyoham-āpnuyām

You seem to bewilder my intelligence with a confused and mingled speech of contradictions; tell me then, decisively, the one way by which I may attain the highest good.

Chapter 3, Verse 3

śrī bhagavān uvāca
loke'smin dvividhā niṣṭhā
purā proktā mayā'nagha
jñāna-yogena sāṅkhyānāṁ
karma-yogena yoginām

The Lord says: In this world there is a two-fold path as I have said before, O sinless one: Jyaana Yoga for the sankhyans and Karma Yoga for the yogis.

Chapter 3, Verse 4

na karmaṇām anārambhān
naiṣkarmyaṁ puruṣo'śnute
na ca saṁnyasanād-eva
siddhiṁ samādhigacchati

No one achieves freedom from karma by abstaining from works, and no one ever attains perfection by mere renunciation of works.

Chapter 3, Verse 5

na hi kaścit kṣaṇam-api
jātu tiṣṭhaty-akarma-kṛt
kāryate hy-avaśaḥ karma
sarvaḥ prakṛti-jair guṇaiḥ

For none stands even for a moment not doing work. Everyone is helplessly made to do action by the modes born of Prakriti.

Chapter 3, Verse 6

**karmendriyāṇi saṁyamya
ya āste manasā smaran
indriyārthān vimūḍhātmā
mithyācāraḥ sa ucyate**

Who controls the organs of action, but continues in his mind to remember and dwell upon the objects of sense, such a man has bewildered himself with false notions of self- discipline.

Chapter 3, Verse 7

**yastv-indriyāṇi manasā
niyamyārabhate 'rjuna
karmendriyaiḥ karma-yogam
asaktaḥ sa viśiṣyate**

But one who, subduing the senses by the mind, O Arjuna, begins to practice Karma Yoga through the organs of action and who is free from attachment, excels.

Chapter 3, Verse 8

**niyataṁ kuru karma tvaṁ
karma jyāyo hy akarmaṇaḥ
śarīra-yātrā'pi ca te
na prasiddhyed akarmaṇaḥ**

You must perform your obligatory duties, for action is superior to non-action (meditation). For not even the maintenance of the body is possible by inaction.

Chapter 3, Verse 9

yajñārthāt karmaṇo'nyatra
loko'yaṁ karma bandhanaḥ
tad-arthaṁ karma kaunteya
mukta saṅgas-samācara

By doing works other than for sacrifice, this world of men is in bondage to these works; perform your actions as sacrifice, O Arjuna, becoming free from all attachment.

Chapter 3, Verse 10

saha yajñāiḥ prajāḥ sṛṣṭvā
purovāca prajāpatiḥ
anena prasaviṣyadhvam
eṣa vo'stviṣṭa kāmadhuk

In the beginning, the Lord of all beings, created humans along with the sacrifice, saying: 'By this shall you prosper; this shall be the cow of plenty granting all your desires.'

Chapter 3, Verse 11

devān bhāvayetānena
te devā bhāvayantu vaḥ
parasparaṁ bhāvayantaḥ
śreyaḥ paramavāpsyatha

By this, may you nurture the gods, and the gods will nurture you in return. Thus, nurturing one another, you will obtain the highest good.

Chapter 3, Verse 12

iṣṭān-bhogān-iha vo devā
dāsyante yajñā-bhāvitāḥ
tair-dattān apradāyaibhyo
yo bhuṅkte stena eva saḥ

The gods, pleased by sacrifice, will bestow on you the enjoyments you desire. One who enjoys the bounty of the gods without offering them anything in return, is verily a thief.

Chapter 3, Verse 13

yajñā-śiṣṭāśinaḥ santo
mucyante sarva kilbiṣaiḥ
bhuñjate te tvaghaṁ pāpā
ye pacantyātma kāraṇāt

The good who eat what is left from the sacrifice, are released from all sin; but evil are they who cook the food for their own sake.

Chapter 3, Verses 14-15

annād-bhavanti būtāni
parjanyād-anna-saṁbhavaḥ
yajñād-bhavati parjanyo
yajñāḥ karma samud-bhavaḥ

karma brahmod-bhavaṁ viddhi
brahmākṣara samudbhavam
tasmāt sarva-gataṁ brahma
nityaṁ yajñe pratiṣṭhitam

From food arise all beings; from rain, food is produced; from sacrifice comes rain; and sacrifice is achieved through activity. Know that activity springs from Brahman and Brahman arises from the imperishable Self; therefore, the all-pervading 'Brahman' is ever-established in sacrifice.

Chapter 3, Verse 16

evaṁ pravartitaṁ cakraṁ
nānu vartayatīha yaḥ
aghāyur-indriyā rāmo
moghaṁ pārtha sa jīvati

One who does not follow this cycle thus set in motion, lives in error, revelling in the senses, he lives in vain O Arjuna.

Chapter 3, Verse 17

yastvātma-ratir-eva syād
ātma tṛptaśca mānavaḥ
ātmanyeva ca santuṣṭas
tasya kāryaṁ na vidyate

But the man whose delight is in the Self and who is satisfied with the enjoyment of the Self and is content in the Self, for him there exists no work that needs to be done.

Chapter 3, Verse 18

naiva tasya kṛtenārtho
nākṛteneha kaścana
na cāsya sarva-bhūteṣu
kaścid artha vyapāśrayaḥ

He has no object here to be gained by action done and none to be gained by action undone; he has no dependence on all these existences for any object to be gained.

Chapter 3, Verse 19

tasmād asaktaḥ satataṁ
kāryaṁ karma samācara
asakto hyācaran karma
param-āpnoti pūruṣaḥ

Therefore, without attachment, perform ever the work that is to be done, for it is by doing work without attachment that man attains to the highest.

Chapter 3, Verse 20

karmaṇaiva hi saṁsiddhim
āsthitā janakādayaḥ
loka saṅgraham-evāpi
saṁpaśyan kartum arhasi

Verily, by Karma Yoga alone did Janaka and others reach perfection. Indeed, you should act, bearing in mind the welfare of the world.

Chapter 3, Verse 21

yadyad-ācarati śreṣṭhah
tat-tad-evetaro janaḥ
sa yat pramāṇaṁ kurute
lokas-tad-anuvartate

Whatever an eminent person does, other people also do; whatever standard he sets, the world follows it.

Chapter 3, Verse 22

na me pārthāsti kartavyaṁ
triṣu lokeṣu kiñcana
nānavāptam-avāptavyaṁ
varta eva ca karmaṇi

For Me, O Arjuna, there is nothing in all the three worlds which ought to be done, nor is there anything lacking that ought to be acquired - yet I continually engage in action.

Chapter 3, Verses 23-24

yadi hyahaṁ na varteyaṁ
jātu karmaṇyatandritaḥ
mama vartmānuvartante
manuṣyāḥ pārtha sarvaśaḥ

utsīdeyur-ime lokā
na kuryaṁ karma ced aham
saṅkarasya ca kartā syām
upahanyām-imāḥ prajāḥ

For if I did not continue to engage Myself in action, unwearied, O Arjuna, humankind would follow My example. These worlds would perish if I did not perform action; I would be the author of confusion and the cause of destruction of these beings.

Chapter 3, Verse 25

saktāḥ karmaṇy-avidvāṁso
yathā kurvanti bhārata
kuryād-vidvāṁs-tathāsaktaḥ
cikīrṣur loka-saṅgraham

Just as the ignorant act with attachment to their work, O Arjuna, so should the wise act without any attachment, and only for the welfare of the world.

Chapter 3, Verse 26

**na buddhi-bhedaṁ janayed
ajñānāṁ karma-saṅginām
joṣayet sarva karmāṇi
vidvān yuktaḥ samācaran**

The wise should not confuse the minds of the ignorant who are attached to work; rather himself performing work with devotion, he should inspire others to do likewise.

Chapter 3, Verse 27

**prakṛteḥ kriyamāṇāni
guṇaiḥ karmāṇi sarvaśaḥ
ahaṅkāra vimūḍhātmā
kartā'ham-iti manyate**

While all actions are being entirely done by the gunas of Prakriti, he whose self is bewildered by egoism thinks that it is his 'I' which is acting.

Chapter 3, Verse 28

**tattva-vittu mahābāho
guṇa-karma-vibhāgayoḥ
guṇā guṇeṣu vartanta
iti matvā na sajjate**

But one, O mighty-armed, who knows the true principles of the divisions of the gunas and of works, realises that it is the gunas which are acting and reacting on each other and is not caught in them by attachment.

Chapter 3, Verse 29

prakṛter-guṇa saṁmūḍhāḥ
sajjante guṇa-karmasu
tān-akṛtsna vido mandān
kṛtsnavinna vicālayet

Those who are deluded by the gunas of Prakriti are attached to the functions of the gunas, but one of perfect knowledge should not unsettle the ignorant who do not know the whole truth.

Chapter 3, Verse 30

mayi sarvāṇi karmāṇi
sanyasyādhyātma-cetasā
nirāśīr-nir-mamo bhūtvā
yudhyasva vigata-jvaraḥ

Dedicating all your actions to Me with a mind centred in the Self, free from desire and selfishness, free from hotheadedness, do you engage in battle.

Chapter 3, Verses 31-32

ye me matam idaṁ nityam
anu-tiṣṭhanti mānavāḥ
śraddhāvanto'nasūyanto
mucyante te'pi karmabhiḥ

ye tvetad abhyasūyanto
nānutiṣṭhanti me matam
sarva jñāna vimūḍhāṁstān
viddhi naṣṭān acetasaḥ

Those who, having faith and not trusting to the critical intelligence, constantly follow this teaching of Mine, they too are released from the bondage of works. But those who find fault with My teaching and act not upon them, are of an unripe mind, bewildered in all knowledge and fated to be destroyed.

Chapter 3, Verse 33

sadṛśaṁ ceṣṭate svasyāḥ
prakṛter-jñānavān api
prakṛtiṁ yānti bhūtāni
nigrahaḥ kiṁ kariṣyati

Even an enlightened person acts in conformity to his own nature; beings follow their nature; what will restraint accomplish?

Chapter 3, Verse 34

indriyasyendriyasyārthe
rāga-dveṣau vyavasthitau
tayor-na vaśam āgacchet
tau hyasya paripanthinau

Attachment and aversion for sense objects abide in the sense-organs; let none come under their sway for they are the obstacles of the soul in its path.

Chapter 3, Verse 35

śreyān sva-dharmo viguṇaḥ
para-dharmāt svanuṣṭhitāt
sva-dharme nidhanaṁ śreyaḥ
para-dharmo bhayāvahaḥ

Better is one's own duty, though devoid of merit, than the duty of another well-done. Better is death in one's own duty; the duty of another is fraught with danger.

Chapter 3, Verse 36

arjuna uvāċa
atha kena prayukto'yaṁ
pāpaṁ carati pūruṣaḥ
anicchann-api vārṣṇeya
balādiva niyojitaḥ

Arjuna says: But if there is no fault in following our nature, what is this in us that drives a man to sin, as if by force, even against his own struggling will, O Krishna?

Chapter 3, Verse 37

śrī bhagavān uvāca
kāma eṣa krodha eṣa
rajoguṇa samudbhavaḥ
mahāśano mahā-pāpmā
viddhyenam-iha vairiṇam

The Lord says: It is desire, it is anger, born of the guna of rajas, all devouring, and impeller to sin. Know this to be the foe here.

Chapter 3, Verse 38

dhūmenāvriyate vahniḥ
yathādarśo malena ca
yatholbenāvṛto garbhaḥ
tathā tenedam-āvṛtam

As a fire is covered over by smoke, as a mirror by dust, as an embryo is wrapped by the amnion, so is this world enveloped by desire.

Chapter 3, Verse 39

āvṛtaṁ jñānam etena
jñānino nitya vairiṇā
kāma-rūpeṇa kaunteya
duṣpūreṇānalena ca

Wisdom is obscured by this constant enemy of the wise, O Arjuna, which is as insatiable as fire.

Chapter 3, Verse 40

indriyāṇi mano buddhiḥ
asyādhiṣṭhānam-ucyate
etair-vimohayaty-eṣa
jñānam-āvṛtya dehinam

The senses, mind and intellect are the seats of desires. Desires veil knowledge and bewilder the embodied soul.

Chapter 3, Verse 41

tasmāt-tvam-indriyāṇyādau
niyamya bharatarṣabha
pāpmānaṁ prajahi hyenaṁ
jñāna vijñāna nāśanam

Therefore, O Arjuna, controlling the senses first, slay desire, this deluding thing that destroys both knowledge and discrimination.

Chapter 3, Verse 42

indriyāṇi parāṇy āhuḥ
indriyebhyaḥ paraṁ manaḥ
manas-astu parā buddhiḥ
yo buddheḥ paratas-tu saḥ

It is said that the senses are supreme, but the mind is superior to the senses, the intellect is superior to the mind, and greater than the intellect is the Self.

Chapter 3, Verse 43

evaṁ buddheḥ paraṁ buddhvā
saṁstabhyātmānam ātmanā
jahi śatruṁ mahā-bāho
kāma-rūpaṁ durāsadam

Thus, knowing that which is greater than the intellect and fixing the mind with the help of the intellect in Karma Yoga, O Arjuna, slay this enemy in the form of desire, which is difficult to overcome.

hariḥ oṁ tat sat
iti śrīmad bhagavad gītā sūpaniṣatsu
brahma vidyāyāṁ yoga śāstre śrī kṛṣṇārjuna
saṁvāde karma yogaḥ nāma tṛtīyo 'dhyāyaḥ

Thus ends Chapter 3: Karma Yoga, from the dialogue between Sri Krishna and Arjuna in the *Upanishad* known as *Shreemad Bhagavad Gita*, the science of the Absolute, the yoga shastra.

CHAPTER 4
JYAANA VIBHAAGA YOGA

atha caturtho 'dhyāyaḥ

Here begins the fourth chapter

Chapter 4, Verse 1

śrī bhagavān uvāca
imaṁ vivasvate yogaṁ
proktavān aham avyayam
vivasvān manave prāha
manur-ikṣvākave'bravīt

The Lord says: This imperishable yoga I gave to Vivasvan (the Sun-god); Vivasvan gave it to Manu (the father of men); Manu gave it to Ikshvaku (the founder of the Solar dynasty.)

Chapter 4, Verse 2

evaṁ paramparā prāptam
imaṁ rāja-rṣayo viduḥ
sa kāleneha mahatā
yogo naṣṭaḥ parantapa

And so it came down from royal sage to royal sage till it was lost in the great lapse of time, O Parantapa.

Chapter 4, Verse 3

sa evāyaṁ mayā te'dya
yogaḥ proktaḥ purātanaḥ
bhakto'si me sakhā ceti
rahasyaṁ hyetad-uttamam

This same ancient and original Yoga has today been declared to you by Me, for you are My devotee and My friend; this is the highest secret.

Chapter 4, Verse 4

arjuna uvāca
aparaṁ bhavato janma
paraṁ janma vivasvataḥ
katham etad vijānīyāṁ
tvam ādau proktavān iti

Arjuna says: The Sun-god was one of the first-born beings (the ancestor of the Solar dynasty) and You are only now born into the world; how am I to comprehend that You declared it to him in the beginning of time?

Chapter 4, Verse 5

śrī bhagavān uvāca
bahūni me vyatītāni
janmāni tava cārjuna
tānyahaṁ veda sarvāṇi
na tvaṁ vettha paraṅtapa

The Lord says: Many are My lives that are past, and yours also, O Arjuna; all of them I know, but you know them not, O scourge of your foes.

Chapter 4, Verse 6

ajo'pi sann-avyayātmā
bhūtānām īśvaro'pi san
prakṛtiṁ svām-adhiṣṭhāya
saṁbhavāmy-ātma māyayā

Though I am the unborn, though I am imperishable in My Self-Existence, though I am the Lord of all existences, yet I stand upon My own Nature and I come into birth by My Self-Maya.

Chapter 4, Verse 7

yadā yadā hi dharmasya
glānir-bhavati bhārata
abhyutthānam-adharmasya
tadā'tmānaṁ sṛjāmy-aham

Whenever there is the fading of the dharma, like nowadays, and the uprising of unrighteousness, then I bring Myself forth into birth.

Chapter 4, Verse 8

paritrāṇāya sādhūnāṁ
vināśāya ca duṣkṛtām
dharma saṁsthāpan-ārthāya
saṁbhavāmi yuge yuge

For the deliverance of the good, for the destruction of the evil-doers, for the enthroning of the right, I am born from age to age.

Chapter 4, Verse 9

janma karma ca me divyam
evaṁ yo vetti tattvataḥ
tyaktvā dehaṁ punar-janma
naiti māmeti so'rjuna

Whosoever thus knows in truth My divine birth and deeds O Arjuna, is not reborn again, and after leaving the body comes to Me.

Chapter 4, Verse 10

vīta rāga-bhaya-krodhā
man mayā mām upāśritāḥ
bahavo jñāna tapasā
pūtā mad-bhāvam āgatāḥ

Freed from desire, fear and anger, absorbed in Me, taking refuge in Me, purified by the austerity of knowledge, many have attained My state.

Chapter 4, Verse 11

ye yathā māṁ prapadyante
tāṁs-tathaiva bhajāmy-aham
mama vartmānuvartante
manuṣyāḥ pārtha sarvaśaḥ

As men approach Me or seek Me, so I accept them to My Love; men follow in every way My path, O Arjuna.

Chapter 4, Verse 12

kāṅkṣantaḥ karmaṇāṁ siddhiṁ
yajanta iha devatāḥ
kṣipraṁ hi mānuṣe loke
siddhir-bhavati karmajā

They who desire the fulfilment of their works on Earth, sacrifice to the gods, because the fulfilment that is born of works is very swift and easy in the human world.

Chapter 4, Verse 13

cātur-varṇyaṁ mayā sṛṣṭaṁ
guṇa karma vibhāgaśaḥ
tasya kartāram api māṁ
viddhy-akartāram avyayam

The system of four castes was generated by Me according to the division of gunas and karma. Though I am the generator, know Me as a non-agent and immutable.

Chapter 4, Verse 14

na māṁ karmāṇi limpanti
na me karma phale spṛhā
iti māṁ yo'bhijānāti
karmabhir-na sa badhyate

Actions do not taint Me, nor have I desire for the fruits of action; he who thus knows Me is not bound by karma.

Chapter 4, Verse 15

evaṁ jñātvā kṛtaṁ karma
pūrvair-api mumukṣubhiḥ
kuru karmaiva tasmāt tvaṁ
pūrvaiḥ pūrvataraṁ kṛtam

Having known this, the ancient seekers for liberation also performed action. Therefore, you also should engage in action alone, as the ancients did in days gone past.

Chapter 4, Verse 16

kiṁ karma kim akarmeti
kavayo'py-atra mohitāḥ
tatte karma pravakṣyāmi
yaj-jñātvā mokṣyase'śubhāt

What is action and what is inaction, as to this, even the sages are perplexed and deluded. I will declare to you that kind of action by the knowledge of which you shall be released from all suffering.

Chapter 4, Verse 17

karmaṇo hyapi boddhavyaṁ
boddhavyaṁ ca vikarmaṇaḥ
akarmaṇaśca boddhavyaṁ
gahanā karmaṇo-gatiḥ

For verily one must understand the nature of action (karma), and the nature of prohibited action (vikarma) as also the nature of non-action (akarma) - profound indeed is the way of action.

Chapter 4, Verse 18

karmaṇya karma yaḥ paśyed
akarmaṇi ca karma yaḥ
sa buddhimān manuṣyeṣu
sa yuktaḥ kṛtsna karma-kṛt

He who sees non-action in action and also action in non-action is wise among people. He is fit for liberation and has concluded all actions.

Chapter 4, Verse 19

yasya sarve samārambhāḥ
kāma saṅkalpa varjitāḥ
jñānāgni dagdha karmāṇāṁ
tam āhuḥ paṇḍitaṁ budhāḥ

Whose undertakings are free from desire, whose works are burned up by the fire of knowledge, him the wise have called a sage.

Chapter 4, Verse 20

tyaktvā karma phalā-saṅgaṁ
nitya tṛpto nirāśrayaḥ
karmaṇy-abhi-pravṛtto'pi
naiva kiñcit karoti saḥ

Having abandoned all attachment to the fruits of his works, ever satisfied without any kind of dependence, he does nothing, though (through his nature) he engages in action.

Chapter 4, Verse 21

nirāśīr yatacitt-ātmā
tyakta sarva parigrahaḥ
śarīraṁ kevalaṁ karma
kurvan-nāpnoti kilbiṣam

He has no personal hopes; he does not seize on things as his personal possessions; his mind and body are under perfect control; performing action by the body alone, he does not commit sin.

Chapter 4, Verse 22

yadṛcchālābha santuṣṭo
dvandvātito vimatsaraḥ
samaḥ siddhāvasiddhau ca
kṛtvāpi na nibadhyate

He who is satisfied with whatever gain comes to him, who has passed beyond the dualities, is jealous of none, and is equal in failure and success, is not bound even when he acts.

Chapter 4, Verse 23

gata-saṅgasya muktasya
jñānāvasthita cetasaḥ
yajñāyā-carataḥ karma
samagraṁ pravilīyate

When a man who is liberated, free from attachment, with his mind, heart and spirit firmly founded in the knowledge of the Self, does works as sacrifice, all his work is dissolved.

Chapter 4, Verse 24

brahmārpaṇaṁ brahma-havir
brahmāgnau brahmaṇā hutam
brahmaiva tena gantavyaṁ
brahma karma samādhinā

Brahman is the instrument, Brahman is the oblation; by Brahman is the oblation offered into the fire of Brahman; Brahman alone is to be reached by one who meditates on Brahman in one's works.

Chapter 4, Verse 25

daivam-evāpare yajñāṁ
yoginaḥ paryupāsate
brahmāgnāv-apare yajñāṁ
yajñenaivopa-juhvati

Some yogis resort only to sacrificing to the gods. Others offer sacrifice into the fire of Brahman solely by means of sacrifice.

Chapter 4, Verse 26

śrotrādīn-indriyāṇy-anye
saṁyamāgniṣu juhvati
śabdādīn-viṣayān-anya
indriyāgniṣu juhvati

Some offer hearing and the other senses into the fires of control. Others offer sound and the other objects of sense into the fires of their senses.

Chapter 4, Verse 27

sarvāṇīndriya karmāṇi
prāṇa karmāṇi cāpare
ātma-saṁyama yogāgnau
juhvati jñāna-dīpite

Some offer the functions of the senses and the activity of the vital energy (prana) as oblation into the fire of the yoga of the controlled mind, kindled by knowledge.

Chapter 4, Verse 28

dravya yajñās-tapo yajñā
yoga yajñās-tathā'pare
svādhyāya-jñāna yajñāśca
yatayaḥ saṁśita vratāḥ

Others again offer material objects, tapas and yoga as sacrifice, while others, being self-restrained and of rigid vows, offer their scriptural study and knowledge as sacrifice.

Chapter 4, Verses 29-30

apāne juhvati prāṇaṁ
prāṇe'pānaṁ tathā'pare
prāṇāpāna-gatī ruddhvā
prāṇāyāma parāyaṇāḥ

apare niyatāhārāḥ
prāṇān prāṇeṣu juhvati
sarve'pyete yajña-vido
yajña kṣapita kalmaṣāḥ

Others again who are devoted to controlling the breath, having restrained the prana (the incoming breath) and apana (the outgoing breath), pour as sacrifice prana into apana and apana into prana.

Chapter 4, Verse 31

yajña-śiṣṭāmṛta bhujo
yānti brahmā sanātanam
nāyaṁ loko'sty-ayajñasya
kuto'nyaḥ kurusattama

They who enjoy the nectar of immortality left over from the sacrifice, attain to the eternal Brahman; this world is not for him who does not sacrifice, how then any other world?

Chapter 4, Verse 32

evaṁ bahu vidhā yajña
vitatā brahmaṇo mukhe
karmajān viddhi tān sarvān
evaṁ jñātvā vimokṣyase

Therefore many forms of sacrifice have been extended from the mouth of Brahman. Know that all these are born of work. Knowing that, you shall be free.

Chapter 4, Verse 33

śreyān dravyamayād yajñāt
jñāna yajñaḥ parantapa
sarvaṁ karmākhilaṁ pārtha
jñāne parisamāpyate

The sacrifice of knowledge, O Arjuna, is greater than any material sacrifice. Knowledge is that in which all this action culminates, O Paartha!

Chapter 4, Verse 34

tad viddhi praṇipātena
paripraśnena sevayā
upadekṣayanti te jñānaṁ
jñāninas-tattva-darśinaḥ

Learn that by worshipping the Feet of the Teacher, by questioning and by service, the men of knowledge who have seen the true principles of things, will instruct you in knowledge.

Chapter 4, Verse 35

yaj-jñātvā na punar-moham
evam yāsyasi pāṇḍava
yena bhūtāny-aśeṣeṇa
drakṣyasy-ātman-yatho mayi

Possessing that knowledge, you shall not fall again into the mind's ignorance, O Pandava; for by this, you shall see all existences without exception in the Self, then in Me.

Chapter 4, Verse 36

api ced-asi pāpebhyaḥ
sarvebhyaḥ pāpa-kṛtamaḥ
sarvaṁ jñāna plavenaiva
vṛjinaṁ santariṣyasi

Even if you are the greatest doer of sin beyond all sinners, you shall cross over all the crookedness of evil in the ship of knowledge.

Chapter 4, Verse 37

yathaidhāṁsi samiddho'gnih
bhasmasāt kurute'rjuna
jñānāgniḥ sarva karmāṇi
bhasmasāt kurute yathā

As a kindled fire turns its fuel to ashes, O Arjuna, so the fire of knowledge turns all karma to ashes.

Chapter 4, Verse 38

na hi jñānena sadṛśaṁ
pavitram iha vidyate
tat-svayaṁ yoga saṁsiddhiḥ
kālenātmani vindati

There is nothing in the world equal in purity to knowledge; the man who is perfected by yoga, finds it of himself in the Self in the course of time.

Chapter 4, Verse 39

śraddhāvāṁ llabhate jñānaṁ
tatparaḥ saṁyatendriyaḥ
jñānaṁ labdhvā parāṁ śāntim
acireṇādhigacchati

He who has faith, who has conquered and controlled the mind and senses, who has fixed his whole conscious being on the supreme reality, he attains knowledge; and having attained knowledge, he goes swiftly to the supreme peace.

Chapter 4, Verse 40

ajñāś-cāśraddhānaśca
saṁśayātmā vinaśyati
nāyaṁ loko'sti na paro
na sukhaṁ saṁśayātmanaḥ

The ignorant who has not faith and is full of doubt goes to perdition; neither this world, nor the supreme world nor any happiness, is for the soul full of doubts.

Chapter 4, Verse 41

yoga-saṁnyasta karmāṇaṁ
jñāna saṁcchinna saṁśayam
ātmavantaṁ na karmāṇi
nibadhnanti dhanañjaya

He who has destroyed all doubt by knowledge and has by yoga given up all works and is in possession of the Self, is not bound by his karma, O Dhananjaya.

Chapter 4, Verse 42

tasmād-ajñāna saṁbhūtaṁ
hṛtsthaṁ jñānāsinātmanaḥ
cchittvainaṁ saṁśayaṁ yogam
ātiṣṭhottiṣṭha bhārata

Therefore arise, O Bharata, and resort constantly to yoga, having cut away with the sword of knowledge this perplexity born of ignorance.

hariḥ oṁ tat sat
iti śrīmad bhagavad gītā sūpaniṣatsu
brahma vidyāyāṁ yoga śāstre śrī kṛṣṇārjuna
saṁvāde jñāna vibhāga yogaḥ nāma
caturtho 'dhyāyaḥ

Thus ends Chapter 4: Jyaana Vibhaaga Yoga, from the dialogue between Sri Krishna and Arjuna in the *Upanishad* known as *Shreemad Bhagavad Gita*, the science of the Absolute, the yoga shastra.

CHAPTER 5
KARMA SANNYASA YOGA

atha pañcamo 'dhyāyaḥ

Here begins the fifth chapter

Chapter 5, Verse 1

arjuna uvāca
saṁnyāsaṁ karmaṇāṁ kṛṣṇa
punar-yogaṁ ca śaṁsasi
yac-chreya etayor-ekaṁ
tan-me brūhi suniścitam

Arjuna says: You declare to me the renunciation of works, O Krishna, and yet You again declare to me Karma Yoga; which one is the better way? Tell me with a clear decisiveness.

Chapter 5, Verse 2

śrī bhagavān uvāca
saṁnyāsaḥ karma yogaśca
niḥśreyasakarāv-ubhau
tayos-tu karma saṁnyāsāt
karma-yogo viśiṣyate

The Lord says: Renunciation and Karma Yoga both bring about the soul's salvation: but of these two paths, Karma Yoga is held to be above the renunciation of works.

Chapter 5, Verse 3

jñeyaḥ sa nitya saṁnyāsī
yo na dveṣṭi na kāṅkṣati
nir-dvandvo hi mahābāho
sukhaṁ bandhāt-pramucyate

Even when he is doing action, he should always be known as a sannyasin who neither dislikes nor desires; free from the dualities, he is easily and happily released from bondage.

Chapter 5, Verse 4

sāṅkhya-yogau pṛthag-bālāḥ
pravadanti na paṇḍitāḥ
ekam-apy-āsthitaḥ samyak
ubhayor-vindate phalam

Children speak of Sankhya Yoga and yoga of action as being different from each other, but not the wise; if a man fully applies himself to one of them, he gets the fruit of both.

Chapter 5, Verse 5

yat-sāṅkhyaiḥ prāpyate sthānaṁ
tad-yogair-api gamyate
ekaṁ sāṅkhyaṁ ca yogaṁ ca
yaḥ paśyati sa paśyati

The status which is attained by Sankhya Yoga, the men of the yoga of action also achieve: he who sees Sankhya Yoga and yoga of action as one, truly sees.

Chapter 5, Verse 6

saṁnyāsas-tu mahābāho
duḥkham-āptum-ayogataḥ
yoga-yukto munir brahma
na cireṇādhigacchati

But renunciation, O mighty-armed, is difficult to attain without the yoga of action; the sage who follows the yoga of action soon attains Brahman.

Chapter 5, Verse 7

yoga-yukto viśuddhātmā
vijitātmā jitendriyaḥ
sarva-bhūtātmā bhūtātmā
kurvann-api na lipyate

He who follows the yoga of action, who has conquered the senses, the pure soul, the master of his Self, whose Self becomes the Self of all existences, even though he does works, he is not involved in them.

Chapter 5, Verses 8-9

naiva kiñcit karomīti
yukto manyeta tattva-vit
paśyaṅ-śṛṇvan spṛśañ jighrann
aśnan gacchan svapaṅ-śvasan

pralapan visṛjan gṛhṇan
unimiṣan nimiṣann-api
indriyāṇīndriyārtheṣu
vartanta iti dhārayan

"I do nothing at all." This is the attitude of a focused knower of the Truth. Even while seeing, hearing, touching, smelling, eating, moving, sleeping, breathing, speaking, releasing, grasping, opening and closing the eyes, he is always aware that he does nothing at all. He knows that the senses operate among sense objects and that he is separate from them.

Chapter 5, Verse 10

brahmaṇyādāya karmāṇi
saṅgaṁ tyaktvā karoti yaḥ
lipyate na sa pāpena
padma-patram ivāmbhasā

Just as water does not cling to the lotus leaf, he who abandons attachment and dedicates all his activities to Brahman, the ultimate Truth, is not stained by sin.

Chapter 5, Verse 11

kāyena manasā buddhyā
kevalair-indriyair-api
yoginaḥ karma kurvanti
saṅgaṁ tyaktvā'tma śuddhaye

Abandoning attachment, the yogis do works with the body, mind, intellect and even the senses for self-purification.

Chapter 5, Verse 12

yuktaḥ karma phalaṁ tyaktvā
śāntim-āpnoti naiṣṭhikīm
ayuktaḥ kāma-kāreṇa
phale sakto nibadhyate

By abandoning attachment to the fruits of action, the soul in union with Brahman attains peace in Brahman. But the soul which is not in union with Brahman is bound by desire and is attached to the fruits.

Chapter 5, Verse 13

sarva karmāṇi manasā
sannyasyāste sukhaṁ vaśī
nava-dvāre pure dehī
naiva kurvan-na kārayan

The embodied soul, perfectly controlling its nature, having renounced all its actions by the mind, sits serenely in its nine-gated city, neither doing nor causing to be done.

Chapter 5, Verse 14

na kartṛtvaṁ na karmāṇi
lokasya sṛjati prabhuḥ
na karma phala saṁyogaṁ
svabhāvastu pravartate

The Lord neither creates the works of the world, nor the state of the doer, nor the joining of the works to the fruit: Nature does this.

Chapter 5, Verse 15

nādatte kasyacit-pāpaṁ
na caiva sukṛtaṁ vibhuḥ
ajñānenāvṛtaṁ jñānaṁ
tena muhyanti jantavaḥ

The omnipresent God Almighty receives neither the sin nor the virtue of any. Knowledge is enveloped in ignorance; thereby creatures are bewildered.

Chapter 5, Verse 16

jñānena tu tad-jñānaṁ
yeṣāṁ nāśitam ātmanaḥ
teṣām ādityavad-jñānaṁ
prakāśayati tat param

Those in whom ignorance is destroyed by Self-Realisation, the Supreme Self glows like the Sun.

Chapter 5, Verse 17

tad-buddhayas tad-ātmānah
tan-niṣṭhās tat-parāyaṇāḥ
gacchanty-apunarāvṛttiṁ
jñāna nirdhūta kalmaṣāḥ

Turning their discerning mind to That, directing their whole conscious being to That, making That their whole aim, the sole object of their devotion, their sins are washed by the waters of knowledge and they go to where there is no return.

Chapter 5, Verse 18

vidyā vinaya saṁpanne
brāhmaṇe gavi hastini
śuni caiva śvapāke ca
paṇḍitāḥ sama-darśinaḥ

Sages see with an equal eye the learned and cultured Brahmin, the cow, the elephant, the dog, the outcast.

Chapter 5, Verse 19

ihaiva tair-jitaḥ sargo
yeṣāṁ sāmye sthitaṁ manaḥ
nir-doṣaṁ hi samaṁ brahma
tasmād brahmaṇi te sthitāḥ

Those whose minds are established in equality have conquered birth and death even here on Earth. They dwell in Brahman. The equal Brahman is faultless.

Chapter 5, Verse 20

na prahṛṣyet priyaṁ prāpya
nodvijet prāpya cāpriyam
sthira-buddhir-asaṁmūḍho
brahma-vid brahmaṇi sthitaḥ

With intelligence stable, unbewildered, the knower of Brahman, living in the Brahman, neither rejoices on obtaining what is pleasant, nor sorrows on obtaining what is unpleasant.

Chapter 5, Verse 21

bāhya-sparśeṣv-asaktātmā
vindaty-ātmani yat sukham
sa brahma-yoga-yuktātmā
sukham akṣayam aśnute

When the soul is no longer attached to the touch of external things, then one finds the true happiness that exists in the Self. Such a person enjoys an imperishable happiness, because his Self is connected by yoga with Brahman.

Chapter 5, Verse 22

ye hi saṁsparśajā bhogā
duḥkha-yonaya eva te
ādy-antavantaḥ kaunteya
na teṣu ramate budhaḥ

Those pleasures that arise from contact with external factors are sources of suffering. They have a beginning and an end. O Arjuna, the wise do not rejoice in them.

Chapter 5, Verse 23

śaknotīhaiva yaḥ soḍhuṁ
prāk-śarīra vimokṣaṇāt
kāma krodhodbhavaṁ vegaṁ
sa yuktaḥ sa sukhī naraḥ

One who is able, even here, before one is released from the body, to resist the impulses arising from desire and anger, is a yogi competent for Self-Realisation, and a happy person.

Chapter 5, Verse 24

yo'ntaḥ sukho'ntarā rāmah
tathāntar jyotir-eva yaḥ
sa yogī brahma-nirvāṇaṁ
brahma-bhūto'dhigacchati

He who has inner happiness, inner ease and repose, and inner Light, that yogi becomes Brahman: he reaches liberation in Brahman, Brahmanirvanam.

Chapter 5, Verse 25

labhante brahma-nirvāṇam
ṛṣayaḥ kṣīṇa kalmaṣāḥ
chinna-dvaidhā yatātmanaḥ
sarva bhūta hite ratāḥ

The sages whose minds are well directed within, who are free from the pairs of opposites, become cleansed of all impurities and attain the bliss of the Brahman; they are devoted to the welfare of all beings.

Chapter 5, Verse 26

kāma krodha viyuktānāṁ
yatīnāṁ yata-cetasām
abhito brahma-nirvāṇaṁ
vartate viditātmanām

To those who are free from desire and anger, whose minds are controlled, who have attained self-mastery, who aspire for Realisation - the great Nirvana is close at hand.

Chapter 5, Verses 27-28

sparśān kṛtvā bahir-bāhyān
cakṣuś-caivāntare bhruvoḥ
prāṇāpānau samau kṛtvā
nāsābhyantara cāriṇau

yatendriya mano-buddhih
munir mokṣa parāyaṇaḥ
vigat-ecchābhaya krodho
yaḥ sadā mukta eva saḥ

Shutting out all external sense objects and concentrating the vision between the eyebrows, making the prana and the apana move equally within the nostrils, controlling the senses, the mind and the intellect, the sage devoted to liberation, who has discarded fear, desire, and anger, is ever free.

Chapter 5, Verse 29

bhoktāraṁ yajña tapasāṁ
sarva loka maheśvaram
suhṛdaṁ sarva-bhūtānāṁ
jñātvā māṁ śāntim-ṛcchati

Knowing Me as the enjoyer of all sacrifices and austerities, as the Supreme Lord of all the worlds, as the Friend of every being, one attains peace.

hariḥ oṁ tat sat
iti śrīmad bhagavad gītā sūpaniṣatsu
brahma vidyāyāṁ yoga śāstre śrī kṛṣṇārjuna
saṁvāde karma saṁnyāsa yogaḥ nāma
pañcamo 'dhyāyaḥ

Thus ends Chapter 5: Karma Sannyasa Yoga, from the dialogue between Sri Krishna and Arjuna in the *Upanishad* known as *Shreemad Bhagavad Gita*, the science of the Absolute, the yoga shastra.

CHAPTER 6
DHYAANA YOGA

atha ṣaṣṭho 'dhyāyaḥ

Here begins the sixth chapter

Chapter 6, Verse 1

śrī bhagavān uvāca
anāśritaḥ karma-phalaṁ
kāryaṁ karma karoti yaḥ
sa saṁnyāsī ca yogī ca
na nir-agnir-na cākriyaḥ

The Lord says: Whoever does the work to be done without attachment to its fruits, he is a sannyasin and a yogi, not the man who doesn't light the sacrificial fire and doesn't do works.

Chapter 6, Verse 2

yaṁ saṁnyāsam iti prāhuḥ
yogaṁ taṁ viddhi pāṇḍava
na hy-asaṁnyasta saṅkalpo
yogī bhavati kaścana

What they have called renunciation (Sannyas), know it to be in truth, yoga, O Pandava, for no one becomes a yogi who has not renounced desire in the mind.

Chapter 6, Verse 3

**āruruksor-muner-yogaṁ
karma kāraṇam ucyate
yogārūḍhasya tasyaiva
śamaḥ kāraṇam ucyate**

For a sage who is ascending the hill of yoga, action is the means: for the same sage, when he has attained the summit of yoga, cessation of all activities is the means.

Chapter 6, Verse 4

**yadā hi nendriyārtheṣu
na karmasv-anuṣajjate
sarva saṅkalpa saṁnyāsī
yogārūḍhas-tad-ocyate**

When one does not get attached to the objects of the senses or to the fruits of actions and has renounced all desire in the mind, he is said to have ascended to the top of yoga.

Chapter 6, Verse 5

**uddhared-ātman-ātmānaṁ
nātmānam avasādayet
ātmaiva hy-ātmano bandhuḥ
ātmaiva ripur-ātmanaḥ**

One should raise oneself by one's own mind and not allow oneself to fall; the mind alone is the friend of the conditioned soul, and also its enemy.

Chapter 6, Verse 6

bandhur-ātmā'tmanas tasya
yenātmaivātmanā jitaḥ
anātmanastu śatrutve
vartetātmaiva śatruvat

The mind is the friend of one who has conquered the mind. But for one whose mind is uncontrolled, the mind remains hostile, like an adversary.

Chapter 6, Verse 7

jitātmanaḥ praśāntasya
paramātmā samāhitaḥ
śītoṣṇa sukha-duḥkheṣu
tathā mānāpamānayoḥ

When one has conquered the mind and attained the calm of perfect self-mastery; when one has transcended the dualities of cold and heat, pleasure and pain, as well as honour and dishonour; then one is firmly established in the Supreme Self.

Chapter 6, Verse 8

jñāna vijñāna tṛptātmā
kūṭastho jitendriyaḥ
yukta ity-ucyate yogī
sama-loṣṭāśma kāñcanaḥ

The yogi, who is established in the knowledge of the Self, tranquil and self-poised, master of his senses, regarding alike earth, stone and gold, is said to be firmly in yoga.

Chapter 6, Verse 9

suhṛn mitrāry-udāsīna
madhyastha dveṣya bandhuṣu
sādhuṣv-api ca pāpeṣu
sama-buddhir viśiṣyate

He who is equal and impartial in action to a friend, an enemy and to a neutral person, also to a sinner and a saint, he excels.

Chapter 6, Verse 10

yogī yuñjīta satatam
ātmānaṁ rahasi sthitaḥ
ekākī yatacittātmā
nirāśīr aparigrahaḥ

Let the yogi continually practise union with the Self, sitting apart and alone, with all desire and idea of possession banished from his mind, self-controlled in his whole being and consciousness.

Chapter 6, Verses 11-12

śucau deśe pratiṣṭhāpya
sthitam-āsanam ātmanaḥ
nāty-ucchritaṁ nāti-nīcaṁ
cailājina kuśottaram

tatraikāgraṁ manaḥ kṛtvā
yata-cittendriya kriyaḥ
upaviśyāsane yuñjyād
yogam-ātma viśuddhaye

He should set his firm seat in a pure spot, neither too high, nor too low, covered with a cloth, a deer skin, and sacred grass; seated there with a concentrated mind, and with the workings of the mental consciousness and the senses under control, he should practise yoga for self-purification.

Chapter 6, Verses 13-14

samaṁ kāya-śiro-grīvaṁ
dhārayann-acalaṁ sthiraḥ
saṁprekṣya nāsikāgraṁ svaṁ
diśaś-cānavalokayan

praśāntātmā vigata-bhīḥ
brahmacāri vrate sthitaḥ
manaḥ saṁyamya mac-citto
yukta āsīta mat-paraḥ

Holding the body, head and neck erect, motionless; the vision drawn in and fixed between the eyebrows; not regarding the regions; the mind kept calm and free from fear; the vow of Brahmacharya observed; the whole controlled mentality turned to Me, one must sit firm in yoga, wholly surrendered to Me.

Chapter 6, Verse 15

yuñjann-evaṁ sadā'tmānaṁ
yogī niyata-mānasaḥ
śāntiṁ nirvāṇa paramāṁ
mat-saṁsthām adhigacchati

Always putting himself in yoga by controlling his mind, the yogi attains to the supreme peace of Nirvana which has its foundation in Me.

Chapter 6, Verse 16

nāty-aśnatas-tu yogo'sti
na caikāntam-anaśnataḥ
na cāti svapnaśīlasya
jāgrato naiva cārjuna

Verily this yoga is not for him who eats too much or sleeps too much; neither is it for him who gives up sleep and food, O Arjuna.

Chapter 6, Verse 17

yuktāhāra vihārasya
yukta ceṣṭasya karmasu
yukta svapnāvabodhasya
yogo bhavati duḥkha-hā

Yoga becomes the destroyer of sorrow for one who is moderate in food and recreation, who is temperate in actions, who is moderate in sleep and wakefulness.

Chapter 6, Verse 18

yadā viniyataṁ cittam
ātmany-evāvatiṣṭhate
niḥspṛhaḥ sarva-kāmebhyo
yukta ity-ucyate sadā

When all the mental consciousness is perfectly controlled and liberated from desire and remains still in the Self, then it is said, "He is verily in yoga."

Chapter 6, Verse 19

yathā dīpo nivātasthe
neṅgate sopamā smṛtā
yogino yata-cittasya
yuñjato yogam-ātmanaḥ

Motionless, like the light of a lamp in a windless place, is the controlled consciousness of the yogi who practises union with the Self.

Chapter 6, Verse 20

yatroparamate cittaṁ
niruddhaṁ yoga-sevayā
yatra caivātmanā'tmānaṁ
paśyann-ātmani tuṣyati

When the mind, restrained by the practice of yoga, attains that infinite bliss, and when seeing the Self by the mind, one is satisfied by the Self alone.

Chapter 6, Verse 21

sukham-ātyantikaṁ yat-tad
buddhi-grāhyam-atīndriyam
vetti yatra na caivāyaṁ
sthitaś-calati tattvataḥ

That in which the soul knows its own true and everlasting bliss, which is perceived by the intelligence and is beyond the senses, established therein, the soul can no longer fall away from the spiritual truth of its being.

Chapter 6, Verse 22

yaṁ labdhvā cāparaṁ lābhaṁ
manyate nādhikaṁ tataḥ
yasmin sthito na duḥkhena
guruṇā'pi vicālyate

That is the greatest of all gains and the treasure beside which all things lose their value. Established therein, he is not disturbed by the assault of mental grief.

Chapter 6, Verse 23

taṁ vidyād duḥkha saṁyoga
viyogaṁ yoga saṁjñitam
sa niścayena yoktavyo
yogo 'nirviṇṇa cetasā

It is the putting away of the contact with pain, the divorce of the mind's marriage from grief. The firm winning of this spiritual bliss is yoga, divine union. This yoga is to be resolutely practised without yielding to any discouragement by difficulty or failure.

Chapter 6, Verses 24-25

saṅkalpa prabhavān kāmān
tyaktvā sarvān-aśeṣataḥ
manasaivendriya-grāmaṁ
viniyamya samantataḥ

śanaiḥ śanairu-paramed
buddhyā dhṛti-gṛhītayā
ātma-saṁsthaṁ manaḥ kṛtvā
na kiñcid-api cintayet

Renouncing without reserve all desires born of the imagination, and completely restraining all the senses by the mind from all directions; very gradually, one should attain tranquillity, with the help of the intellect held by a firm resolution. Having focused the mind on the Self, one should think of nothing else.

Chapter 6, Verse 26

yato yato niścarati
manaś-cañcalam asthiraṁ
tatas-tato niyamyaitad
ātmanyeva vaśaṁ nayet

Whenever the restless and unquiet mind goes forth, it should be controlled and brought into subjection in the Self.

Chapter 6, Verse 27

praśānta manasaṁ hyenaṁ
yoginaṁ sukham-uttamam
upaiti śānta rajasaṁ
brahma-bhūtam akalmaṣam

When the mind is completely quieted, then there comes upon the yogi the stainless, passionless, highest bliss of the soul that has become Brahman.

Chapter 6, Verse 28

yuñjann-evaṁ sadā'tmānaṁ
yogī vigata kalmaṣaḥ
sukhena brahma saṁsparśam
atyantaṁ sukham-aśnute

Thus freed from the stain of passion and putting himself constantly in yoga, the yogi easily and happily enjoys the touch of Brahman which is an unsurpassable bliss.

Chapter 6, Verse 29

sarva-bhūtastham ātmānaṁ
sarva-bhūtāni cātmani
īkṣate yoga-yuktātmā
sarvatra sama-darśanaḥ

The man whose Self is in yoga, sees the Self in all beings and all beings in the Self, is equal-visioned everywhere.

Chapter 6, Verse 30

yo māṁ paśyati sarvatra
sarvaṁ ca mayi paśyati
tasyāhaṁ na praṇaśyāmi
sa ca me na praṇaśyati

He who sees Me everywhere and sees all in Me, to him I do not get lost, nor does he get lost to Me.

Chapter 6, Verse 31

sarva-bhūta-sthitaṁ yo māṁ
bhajaty-ekatvam-āsthitaḥ
sarvathā vartmāno'pi
sa yogī mayi vartate

The yogi who is established in unity, worships Me dwelling in all beings; he abides in Me, howsoever he may live.

Chapter 6, Verse 32

ātmaupamyena sarvatra
samaṁ paśyati yo'rjuna
sukhaṁ vā yadi vā duḥkhaṁ
sa yogī paramo mataḥ

He, O Arjuna, who sees with equality everything in the image of the Self, whether it be grief or happiness, I hold him to be the supreme yogi.

Chapter 6, Verse 33

arjuna uvāca
yo'yaṁ yogas-tvayā proktaḥ
sāmyena madhusūdana
etasyāhaṁ na paśyāmi
cañcalatvāt sthitiṁ sthirām

Arjuna says: This yoga of equanimity, which has been taught by You, O Krishna, I cannot imagine its steady continuance, because of the restlessness of the mind.

Chapter 6, Verse 34

cañcalaṁ hi manaḥ kṛṣṇa
pramāthi balavad-dṛḍham
tasyāhaṁ nigrahaṁ manye
vāyoriva suduṣkaram

Restless indeed is the mind, O Krishna; it is vehement, strong and unconquerable; I see it as hard to control as the wind.

Chapter 6, Verse 35

śrī bhagavān uvāca
asaṁśayaṁ mahābāho
mano dur-nigrahaṁ calam
abhyāsena tu kaunteya
vairāgyeṇa ca gṛhyate

The Lord says: Without doubt, O mighty-armed, the mind is restless and very difficult to restrain; but, O Kaunteya, it may be controlled by constant practice and non-attachment.

Chapter 6, Verse 36

asaṁyatātmanā yogo
duṣprāpa iti me matiḥ
vaśyātmanā tu yatatā
śakyo'vāptum upāyataḥ

If one is not self-controlled, yoga is difficult to attain; but if one is self-controlled, yoga is attained by properly directed efforts.

Chapter 6, Verse 37

arjuna uvāca
ayatiḥ śraddhayopeto
yogāc-calita-mānasaḥ
aprāpya yoga-saṁsiddhiṁ
kāṁ gatiṁ kṛṣṇa gacchati

Arjuna says: He who takes up yoga with faith, but cannot control himself with the mind, wandering away from yoga, failing to attain perfection in yoga, what is his end, O Krishna?

Chapter 6, Verse 38

kaccin-nobhaya-vibhraṣṭaḥ
chinnābhram iva naśyati
apratiṣṭho mahābāho
vimūḍho brahmaṇaḥ pathi

Does he not, O mighty-armed, lose this life of human activity and Brahman Consciousness to which he aspires, and falling from both, perish like a dissolving cloud?

Chapter 6, Verse 39

etan-me saṁśayaṁ kṛṣṇa
chettum arhasy-aśeṣataḥ
tvad-anyaḥ saṁśayasyāsya
chettā na hy-upapadyate

O Krishna, please completely dispel this doubt without leaving any residue, for there is none else than You who can destroy this doubt.

Chapter 6, Verse 40

śrī bhagavān uvāca
pārtha naiveha nāmutra
vināśas tasya vidyate
na hi kalyāṇa-kṛt kaścid
durgatiṃ tāta gacchati

The Lord says: O Arjuna, neither in this life nor hereafter is there destruction for him; never does anyone who practises good, O beloved, come to woe.

Chapter 6, Verse 41

prāpya puṇya-kṛtāṁ lokān
uṣitvā śāśvatīḥ samāḥ
śucināṁ śrīmatāṁ gehe
yoga-bhraṣṭo 'bhijāyate

Having attained the realms of the righteous and dwelt there for many long years, one who has fallen from yoga is born again in the house of the pure and prosperous.

Chapter 6, Verse 42

athavā yoginām eva
kule bhavati dhīmatām
etaddhi durlabhataraṁ
loke janma yadīdṛśam

Or he may be born in the family of a wise yogi; indeed, such a birth is rare to obtain in this world.

Chapter 6, Verse 43

tatra taṁ buddhi saṁyogaṁ
labhate paurva-dehikam
yatate ca tato bhūyaḥ
saṁsiddhau kurunandana

There he recovers the mental state of union with the Divine which he had achieved in his previous life: and with this he again endeavours for perfection, O Arjuna.

Chapter 6, Verse 44

pūrvābhyāsane tenaiva
hriyate hyavaśo'pi saḥ
jijñāsur-api yogasya
śabda-brahmātivartate

By that former practice he is irresistibly carried on. The seeker after the knowledge of yoga goes beyond the range of the *Vedas* and *Upanishads*.

Chapter 6, Verse 45

prayatnād yatamānastu
yogī saṁśuddha-kilbiṣaḥ
aneka-janma saṁsiddhas
tato yāti parāṁ gatim

But the yogi, endeavouring with diligence, purified from sin, perfecting himself through many lives, attains the highest goal.

Chapter 6, Verse 46

tapasvibhyo'dhiko yogī
jñānibhyo'pi mato'dhikaḥ
karmibhyaścādhiko yogī
tasmād yogī bhavārjuna

The yogi is greater than the ascetics, greater than the men of knowledge, greater than the men of works; become then the yogi, O Arjuna.

Chapter 6, Verse 47

yoginām api sarveṣāṁ
mad-gatenāntarātmanā
śraddhāvān bhajate yo māṁ
sa me yuktatamo mataḥ

Of all the yogis, he who with all his inner Self given up to Me, for Me has love and faith, him I hold to be the most united with Me in yoga.

Oṁ tat sat
iti śrīmad bhagavad gītā sūpaniṣatsu
brahma vidyāyāṁ yoga śāstre śrī kṛṣṇārjuna
saṁvāde dhyāna yogaḥ nāma ṣaṣṭho
'dhyāyaḥ

Thus ends Chapter 6: Dhyaana Yoga, from the dialogue between Sri Krishna and Arjuna in the *Upanishad* known as *Shreemad Bhagavad Gita*, the science of the Absolute, the yoga shastra.

CHAPTER 7
JYAANA VIJYAANA YOGA

atha saptamo 'dhyāyaḥ

Here begins the seventh chapter

Chapter 7, Verse 1

śrī bhagavān uvāca
mayyāsakta manāḥ pārtha
yogaṁ yuñjan madāśrayaḥ
asaṁśayaṁ samagraṁ māṁ
yathā jñāsyasi tacchṛṇu

The Lord says: O Paartha, by practising yoga with a mind attached to Me and with Me as the root, you will know Me without any remainder of doubt.

Chapter 7, Verse 2

jñānaṁ te'haṁ savijñānam
idaṁ vakṣyāmy-aśeṣataḥ
yajjñātvā neha bhūyo'nyat
jñātavyam avaśiṣyate

I will speak to you without omission of the essential knowledge, along with all the comprehensive knowledge, knowing which there will be no other thing left to be known.

Chapter 7, Verse 3

manuṣyāṇāṁ sahasreṣu
kaścid yatati siddhaye
yatatām-api siddhānāṁ
kaścin māṁ vetti tattvataḥ

Among thousands of men, perhaps one strives for perfection; among those who strive for perfection, only one may know Me; and among those who know Me, one alone perhaps, knows Me in reality.

Chapter 7, Verse 4

bhūmir-āpo'nalo vāyuḥ
khaṁ mano buddhir-eva ca
ahaṅkāra itīyaṁ me
bhinnā prakṛtir-aṣṭadhā

Earth, water, fire, air, ether, mind, intellect and ego; thus My material Nature (Prakriti) is divided eightfold.

Chapter 7, Verse 5

apareyamitastvanyāṁ
prakṛtiṁ viddhi me parām
jīvabhūtāṁ mahābāho
yayedaṁ dhāryate jagat

This is My inferior Nature. But, O Arjuna, know that My superior Nature is different: it is the life-principle (Jivabhuta or Jivatma), by which this universe is sustained.

Chapter 7, Verse 6

etad-yonīni bhūtāni
sarvāṇītyupadhāraya
ahaṁ kṛtsnasya jagataḥ
prabhavaḥ pralayastathā

Know this to be the womb of all beings. I am the birth of the whole world and also its dissolution.

Chapter 7, Verse 7

mattaḥ parataraṁ nānyat
kiñcid-asti dhanañjayaḥ
mayi sarvam idaṁ protaṁ
sūtre maṇi-gaṇā iva

There is nothing else supreme beyond Me, O Dhananjaya. On Me, all that is here is strung like pearls upon a thread.

Chapter 7, Verse 8

raso'ham-apsu kaunteya
prabhāsmi śaśi-sūryayo
praṇavaḥ sarva vedeṣu
śabdaḥ khe pauruṣaṁ nṛṣu

I am the taste in the water, O Arjuna! I am the radiance in the Sun and the Moon; I am the sacred syllable *OM* in all the *Vedas*; sound in the ether, and the valour in men.

Chapter 7, Verse 9

puṇyo gandhaḥ pṛthivyāṁ ca
tejaścāsmi vibhāvasau
jīvanaṁ sarva bhūteṣu
tapaścāsmi tapasviṣu

I am pure scent in the Earth and the energy of light in fire; I am the life in all existences, I am the ascetic force of those who do asceticism.

Chapter 7, Verse 10

bījaṁ māṁ sarva bhūtānāṁ
viddhi pārtha sanātanaṁ
buddhir-buddhimatām asmi
tejas-tejasvinām aham

Know me to be the Eternal Seed of all existences, O Arjuna. I am the intellect of the intelligent, the energy of the energetic.

Chapter 7, Verse 11

balaṁ balavatāṁ cāhaṁ
kāma-rāga vivarjitam
dharmāviruddho bhūteṣu
kāmo'smi bharatarṣabha

I am the strength of the strong, devoid of desire and liking. I am in beings the desire which is not contrary to dharma, O Lord of the Bharatas.

Chapter 7, Verse 12

ye caiva sāttvikā bhāvā
rājasāstāmasāśca ye
matta eveti tān-viddhi
na tvahaṁ teṣu te mayi

And as for the secondary, subjective becomings of Nature, the bhavah, which are sattvic, rajasic and tamasic, they are verily from Me, but I am not in them: they are in Me.

Chapter 7, Verse 13

tribhir-guṇa-mayair-bhāvair
ebhiḥ sarvam idaṁ jagat
mohitaṁ nābhijānāti
māmebhyaḥ param-avyayam

By these three qualities which are the nature of the gunas, this whole world is bewildered and does not recognise Me, the Supreme, beyond them and imperishable.

Chapter 7, Verse 14

daivī hyeṣā guṇamayī
mama māyā duratyayā
māmeva ye prapadyante
māyāmetāṁ taranti te

This is My Divine Maya of the gunas and it is hard to overcome; those cross beyond it who approach Me.

Chapter 7, Verse 15

na māṁ duṣkṛtino mūḍhāḥ
prapadyante narādhamāḥ
māyayāpahṛta jñānā
āsuraṁ bhāvam āśritāḥ

The evil-doers, souls bewildered, low in the human scale, attain not to Me; for their knowledge is taken away from them by Maya and they resort to the nature of the asura.

Chapter 7, Verse 16

catur-vidhā bhajante māṁ
janāḥ sukṛtino'rjuna
ārto jijñāsur arthārthī
jñānī ca bharatarṣabha

Among the virtuous ones who turn towards Me with devotion, O Arjuna, there are four kinds of bhaktas: the suffering, the seeker for worldly fulfilment, the seeker for knowledge, and those who adore Me with knowledge, O Lord of the Bharatas.

Chapter 7, Verse 17

teṣāṁ jñānī nitya-yukta
eka bhaktir-viśiṣyate
priyo hi jñānino'tyartham
ahaṁ sa ca mama priyaḥ

Of those, the knower who is ever in constant union with the Divine, whose bhakti is all concentrated on Him, is the best: he loves Me perfectly and is My beloved.

Chapter 7, Verse 18

udārāḥ sarva evaite
jñānī tvātmaiva me matam
āsthitaḥ sa hi yuktātmā
māmevānuttamāṁ gatim

Noble are all these without exception. But the knower is verily My Self: for as his highest goal he accepts Me, the Purushottama, with whom he is in union.

Chapter 7, Verse 19

bahūnāṁ janmanām ante
jñānavān māṁ prapadyate
vāsudevaḥ sarvam iti
sa mahātmā sudurlabhaḥ

At the end of many births, the man of knowledge attains to Me. Very rare is the great soul who knows that Vasudeva, the omnipresent Being, is all that is.

Chapter 7, Verse 20

kāmais tais tair hṛta-jñānāḥ
prapadyante'nya-devatāḥ
taṁ taṁ niyamam āsthāya
prakṛtyā niyatāḥ svayā

Controlled by their inherent nature, and deprived of insight by various desires, the worldly-minded resort to other demigods, observing various disciplines.

Chapter 7, Verse 21

yo yo yāṁ yāṁ tanuṁ bhaktaḥ
śraddhayārcitum icchati
tasya tasyācalāṁ śraddhāṁ
tām-eva vidadhāmy-ahaṁ

Whichever manifestation of the Divine any devotee desires to worship with faith - that faith I make unshakeable and firm.

Chapter 7, Verse 22

sa tayā śraddhayā yuktas
tasyārādhanam īhate
labhate ca tataḥ kāmān
mayaiva vihitān hitān

He endowed with faith worships that form, and when by the force of that faith in his worship he gets his desires fulfilled, it is I Myself who (in that form) give these fruits.

Chapter 7, Verse 23

antavattu phalaṁ teṣāṁ
tad bhavaty-alpa medhasām
devān devayajo yānti
mad-bhaktā yānti mām api

But these fruits are temporary, sought after by those who are of petty intelligence and unformed reason. To the demigods go the worshippers of the demigods, but My devotees come to Me.

Chapter 7, Verse 24

avyaktaṁ vyaktim āpannaṁ
manyante mām abuddhayaḥ
paraṁ bhāvam ajānanto
mamāvyayam anuttamam

Petty minds think of Me, the unmanifested, as being limited by manifestation, because they know not My Supreme Nature of being, imperishable, most perfect.

Chapter 7, Verse 25

nāhaṁ prakāśaḥ sarvasya
yoga māyā samāvṛtaḥ
mūḍho'yaṁ nābhijānanti
loko mām ajam avyayam

Nor am I revealed to all, enveloped in My Yogmaya; this bewildered world knows Me not, the unborn, the imperishable.

Chapter 7, Verse 26

vedāhaṁ samatītāni
vartamānāni cārjuna
bhaviṣyāṇi ca bhūtāni
māṁ tu veda na kaścana

I know all beings, O Arjuna, that have been in the past, those now in the present and those yet to come; but no one knows Me.

Chapter 7, Verse 27

icchā-dveṣa samutthena
dvandva mohena bhārata
sarva bhūtāni saṁmohaṁ
sarge yānti parantapa

By the delusion of the dualities which arises from liking and disliking, O Arjuna, all existences in the creation are led into bewilderment.

Chapter 7, Verse 28

yeṣāṁ tvanta-gataṁ pāpaṁ
janānāṁ puṇya-karmaṇām
te dvandva-moha-nirmuktā
bhajante māṁ dṛḍha-vratāḥ

But those men of virtuous deeds, in whom sin has come to an end, they, freed from the delusion of the dualities, worship Me, steadfast in the vow of self-consecration.

Chapter 7, Verse 29

jarā-maraṇa-mokṣayā
mām-āśritya yatanti ye
te brahma tad viduḥ kṛtsnam
adhyātmaṁ karma cākhilam

Those who resort to Me as their refuge, those who turn to Me in their spiritual effort for release from age and death, come to know Brahman and all the integrality of the spiritual nature and the entirety of karma.

Chapter 7, Verse 30

sādhibhūtādhidaivaṁ māṁ
sādhiyajñaṁ ca ye viduḥ
prayāṇa kāle'pi ca māṁ
te vidur yukta cetasaḥ

Because they know Me, and know the material and the Divine Nature of being, and the truth of the Master of sacrifice, they keep knowledge of Me also at the critical moment of their departure from physical existence and at that moment have their whole consciousness in union with Me, the Purushottama.

hariḥ oṁ tat sat
iti śrīmad bhagavad gītā sūpaniṣatsu
brahma vidyāyāṁ yoga śāstre śrī kṛṣṇārjuna
saṁvāde jñāna vijñāna yogaḥ nāma
saptamo 'dhyāyaḥ

Thus ends Chapter 7: Jyaana Vijyaana Yoga, from the dialogue between Sri Krishna and Arjuna in the *Upanishad* known as *Shreemad Bhagavad Gita*, the science of the Absolute, the yoga shastra.

CHAPTER 8
AKSHARA BRAHMA YOGA

atha aṣṭamo 'dhyāyaḥ

Here begins the eighth chapter

Chapter 8, Verse 1

arjuna uvāca
kiṁ tad-brahma kim-adhyātma
kiṁ karma puruṣottama
adhi-bhūtaṁ ca kiṁ proktam
adhi-daivaṁ kim-ucyate

Arjuna says: What is that Brahman (the ultimate reality)? What is Adhyatma (that which is associated with the Self)? What is karma (action)? What is adhibhuta (pertaining to matter)? O Supreme Being, who is Adhidaiva (pertaining to the demigods)?

Chapter 8, Verse 2

adhiyajñaḥ kathaṁ ko'tra
dehe'smin madhusūdana
prayāṇa-kāle ca kathaṁ
jñeyo'si niyatātmabhiḥ

Who is Adhiyajna (the principle of sacrifice) in this body, and how is He the Adhiyajna, O Krishna? And how are You to be known at the time of death by the self-controlled?

Chapter 8, Verse 3

śrī bhagavān uvāca
akṣaraṁ brahma paramaṁ
svabhāvo'dhyātmam-ucyate
bhūta-bhāvodbhava-karo
visargaḥ karma-saṁjñitaḥ

The Lord says: Brahman is the Supreme, indestructible Self (Aksara). One's own material nature (svabhava) is that which dwells with the Self (Adhyatma). The externalised creative force which gives rise to material entities is known as karma.

Chapter 8, Verse 4

adhibhūtaṁ kṣaro bhāvaḥ
puruṣaś-cādhidaivataṁ
adhiyajño'hamevātra
dehe deha-bhṛtāṁ vara

O best of the embodied beings, the physical nature, which is constantly changing, is called adhibhuta, the material manifestation. My omnipresent transcendental aspect, Purusha, the underlying foundation of all the demigods, is called Adhidaiva. And I, the Supreme Lord, represented as the Supersoul in the heart of every embodied being, am called Adhiyajna, the Lord of sacrifice.

Chapter 8, Verse 5

antakāle ca mām-eva
smaran-muktvā kalevaram
yaḥ prayāti sa mad-bhāvaṁ
yāti nāsty-atra saṁśayaḥ

Whoever leaves his body and departs remembering Me at his time of end, comes to My status of Being, that of the Purushottama; there is no doubt of that.

Chapter 8, Verse 6

yaṁ yaṁ vāpi smaran-bhāvaṁ
tyajaty-ante kalevaram
taṁ tam-evaiti kaunteya
sadā tad-bhāva-bhāvitaḥ

Whoever at the end abandons the body, thinking upon any form of being, to that form he attains, O Kaunteya, the form into which the soul was at each moment growing inwardly during the physical life.

Chapter 8, Verse 7

tasmāt sarveṣu kāleṣu
mām-anusmara yudhya ca
mayyarpita mano-buddhiḥ
mām evaiṣyasy-asaṁśayaḥ

Therefore, at all times remember Me and fight, for if your mind and your understanding are always fixed on Me and surrendered to Me, to Me you will surely come.

Chapter 8, Verse 8

abhyāsa-yoga-yuktena
cetasā nānya-gāminā
paramaṁ puruṣaṁ divyaṁ
yāti pārthānucintayan

For it is by always thinking of Him, with a consciousness united with Him, in an undeviating yoga of constant practice, that one comes to the Divine and Supreme Purusha, O Paartha.

Chapter 8, Verses 9-10

kaviṁ purāṇam anuśāsitāram
aṇoraṇīyāṁsam anusmared yaḥ
sarvasya dhātāram acintya-rūpam
āditya varṇaṁ tamasaḥ parastāt

prayāṇa-kāle manasācalena
bhaktyā yukto yoga-balena caiva
bhruvor madhye prāṇam āveśya samyak
sa taṁ paraṁ puruṣam upaiti divyam

This Supreme Self is the Seer, the Ancient of Days, subtler than the subtlest, the Master and Ruler of all existence, who sets in their place in His being all things that are. His form is unthinkable. He is as refulgent as the Sun beyond the darkness. He who thinks upon this Purusha at the time of departure, with a motionless mind, a soul armed with the strength of yoga, a union with God in bhakti, and the life force entirely drawn up and set between the brows in the seat of mystic vision, he attains to this Supreme Divine Purusha.

Chapter 8, Verse 11

yad-akṣaraṁ deva-vido vadanti
viśanti yad-yatayo vītarāgāḥ
yad-icchanto brahmacaryaṁ caranti
tatte padaṁ saṅgraheṇa pravakṣye

This Supreme Soul is the immutable, self-existent Brahman of whom knowers of the *Vedas* speak; this is that into which the doers of asceticism enter when they have gone beyond the affections of the mind of mortality and for the desire of which they practise the control of the bodily passions. That status I will declare to you with brevity.

Chapter 8, Verses 12-13

sarva-dvārāṇi saṁyamya
mano hṛdi nirudhya ca
mūrdhny-ādhāyātmanaḥ prāṇam
āsthito yoga-dhāraṇam

om-ity-ekākṣaraṁ brahma
vyāharan mām-anusmaran
yaḥ prayāti tyajan-dehaṁ
sa yāti paramāṁ gatim

All the doors of the senses closed, the mind shut in into the heart, the life force taken up out of its diffused movement into the head; the intelligence concentrated in the utterance of the sacred syllable *OM* and its conceptive thought in the remembrance of the Supreme Lord, he who goes forth, abandoning the body, attains to the highest status.

Chapter 8, Verse 14

ananya-cetāḥ satataṁ
yo māṁ smarati nityaśaḥ
tasyāhaṁ sulabhaḥ pārtha
nitya-yuktasya yoginaḥ

He who continually remembers Me, thinking of none else, the yogi, O Paartha, who is in constant union with Me, finds Me easy to attain.

Chapter 8, Verse 15

mām-upetya punar-janma
duḥkh-ālayam aśāśvatam
nāpnuvanti mahātmānaḥ
saṁsiddhiṁ paramāṁ gatāḥ

Having come to Me, these great souls come not again to birth, this transient and painful condition of our mortal being; they reach the highest perfection.

Chapter 8, Verse 16

ābrahma bhuvanāllokāḥ
punar-āvartino'rjuna
mām-upetya tu kaunteya
punar-janma na vidyate

All from the highest heavens are subject to rebirth: but, O Kaunteya, there is no rebirth imposed on the soul that comes to Me (the Purushottama).

Chapter 8, Verse 17

sahasra-yuga-paryantam
aharyad brahmaṇo viduḥ
rātriṁ yuga sahasrāntāṁ
te'horātra-vido janāḥ

Those who know the Day of Brahma, a thousand mahayugas in duration, and the night, a thousand mahayugas in ending, they are the knowers of Day and Night.

Chapter 8, Verse 18

avyaktād-vyaktayaḥ sarvāḥ
prabhavanty-ahar-āgame
rātry-āgame pralīyante
tatraivāvyakta saṁjñake

At the coming of the Day, all manifestations are born into being out of the unmanifested; at the coming of the Night, all vanish or are dissolved into it.

Chapter 8, Verse 19

bhūta-grāmaḥ sa evāyaṁ
bhūtvā bhūtvā pralīyate
ratry-āgame'vaśaḥ pārtha
prabhavaty-ahar-āgame

The same multitude of beings comes forth again and again irresistibly, and is withdrawn at the coming of the Night. Once again, it comes forth at the coming of the Day.

Chapter 8, Verse 20

paras-tasmāt tu bhavo 'nyo
'vyakto 'vyaktāt-sanātanaḥ
yaḥ sa sarveṣu bhūteṣu
naśyatsu na vinaśyati

But this unmanifested is not the original divinity of the Being; there is another status of His existence, a supracosmic unmanifested beyond this cosmic non-manifestation, not forced to perish with the perishing of all these existences.

Chapter 8, Verse 21

avyakto 'kṣara ity-uktaḥ
tamāhuḥ paramāṁ gatim
yaṁ prāpya na nivartante
tad-dhāma paramaṁ mama

He is called the unmanifested immutable, Him they speak of as the Supreme Soul and status, and those who attain to Him return not; that is My supreme place of being.

Chapter 8, Verse 22

puruṣaḥ sa paraḥ pārtha
bhaktyā labhyas-tv-ananyayā
yasyāntaḥ sthāni bhūtāni
yena sarvam idaṁ tatam

But that Supreme Purusha has to be won by the bhakta who turns to Him alone, in whom all beings exist and by whom all this world has been extended in space.

Chapter 8, Verse 23

yatra kāle tvanāvṛttim
āvṛttiṁ caiva yoginaḥ
prayātā yānti taṁ kālaṁ
vakṣyāmi bharatarṣabha

O foremost of the Bharatas, I will now declare to you that time wherein departing yogis do not return, and also that time wherein departing they do return.

Chapter 8, Verses 24-25

agnir-jyotir-ahaḥ śuklaḥ
ṣaṇmāsā uttarāyaṇam
tatra prayātā gacchanti
brahma brahma-vido janāḥ

dhūmo rātris-tathā kṛṣṇaḥ
ṣaṇmāsā dakṣiṇāyanam
tatra cāndramasaṁ jyotiḥ
yogī prāpya nivartate

Those who know Brahman, depart this world during the influence of the fiery god, in the light, at an auspicious time, during the time of the waxing Moon or during the six months when the Sun travels in the northern hemisphere. The yogis who depart this world during the night, during the waning Moon or during the six months when the Sun passes to the southern hemisphere, attain the celestial lunar abode, but return again.

Chapter 8, Verse 26

śukla-kṛṣṇe gatī hyete
jagataḥ śāśvate mate
ekayā yāty-anāvṛtim
anyāyāvartate punaḥ

These two paths, the bright and the dark, are said to be everlasting. By the former, one attains the state of non-return, by the other, one returns again.

Chapter 8, Verse 27

naite sṛtī pārtha jānan
yogī muhyati kaścana
tasmāt sarveṣu kāleṣu
yoga-yukto bhavārjuna

The yogi who knows them is not misled into any error: therefore, at all times, be in yoga, O Arjuna.

Chapter 8, Verse 28

vedeṣu yajñeṣu tapaḥsu caiva
dāneṣu yat puṇya-phalaṁ pradiṣṭam
atyeti tat sarvam idaṁ viditvā
yogī paraṁ sthānam upaiti cādyam

The fruit of praiseworthy deeds declared in the *Vedas*, sacrifices, austerities and charitable gifts, the yogi passes all these by, having known this, and attains the supreme and sempiternal status.

hariḥ oṁ tat sat
iti śrīmad bhagavad gītā sūpaniṣatsu
brahma vidyāyāṁ yoga śāstre śrī kṛṣṇārjuna
saṁvāde akṣara brahma yogaḥ nāmāṣṭamo
'dhyāyaḥ

Thus ends Chapter 8: Akshara Brahma Yoga, from the dialogue between Sri Krishna and Arjuna in the *Upanishad* known as *Shreemad Bhagavad Gita*, the science of the Absolute, the yoga shastra.

CHAPTER 9
RAAJAVIDYAA RAAJAGUHYA YOGA

atha navamo 'dhyāyaḥ

Here begins the ninth chapter

Chapter 9, Verse 1

śrī bhagavān uvāca
idaṁ tu te guhyatamaṁ
pravakṣyāmy-anasūyave
jñānaṁ vijñāna sahitaṁ
yaj-jñātvā mokṣyase'śubhāt

The Lord Supreme, Narayana Himself says: What I am going to tell you, who is without fault, is the most secret thing of all, the essential knowledge and wisdom, knowing which you will be released from the miseries of material existence.

Chapter 9, Verse 2

rāja-vidyā rāja-guhyaṁ
pavitram idam uttamam
pratyakṣāvagamaṁ dharmyaṁ
su-sukhaṁ kartum avyayam

This is the king-knowledge, the king-secret: it is a pure and supreme Light which one can verify by direct spiritual experience, it is the right and just knowledge, the very law of being. It is easy to practise and imperishable.

Chapter 9, Verse 3

aśraddadhānāḥ puruṣā
dharmasyāsya parantapa
aprāpya māṁ nivartante
mṛtyu-saṁsāra vartmani

The soul that fails to have faith in the higher Truth and law, O Arjuna, not attaining to Me, must return to the path of ordinary mortal living.

Chapter 9, Verse 4

mayā tatam idaṁ sarvaṁ
jagad avyakta mūrtinā
mat-sthāni sarva bhūtāni
na cāhaṁ teṣv-avasthitaḥ

All this universe has been extended by Me in the ineffable mystery of My Being; all existences are in Me, but I am not in them.

Chapter 9, Verse 5

**na ca mat-sthāni bhūtāni
paśya me yogam aiśvaram
bhūta-bhṛnna ca bhūtastho
mamātmā bhūtabhāvanaḥ**

And yet everything that is created doesn't rest in Me. Behold the mystery of My Divine Yoga (Energy). My Will alone supports all beings and constitutes their existence.

Chapter 9, Verse 6

**yathākāśa-sthito nityaṁ
vāyuḥ sarvatrago mahān
tathā sarvāṇi bhūtāni
mat-sthānīty-upadhāraya**

As the wind blowing everywhere dwells in the etheric, so too all existences dwell in Me: that is how you have to conceive it.

Chapter 9, Verse 7

**sarva bhūtāni kaunteya
prakṛtiṁ yānti māmikām
kalpa-kṣaye punas-tāni
kalpādau visṛjāmy-aham**

All existences, O Kaunteya, return into My Divine Nature in the lapse of the cycle (kalpa); at the beginning of the new cycle, again I send them forth.

Chapter 9, Verse 8

prakṛtiṁ svām-avaṣṭabhya
visṛjāmi punaḥ punaḥ
bhūta-grāmam imaṁ kṛtsnam
avaśaṁ prakṛter-vaśāt

Animating My own Nature (Prakriti), I create all this multitude of existences, all helplessly subject to the control of Nature.

Chapter 9, Verse 9

na ca māṁ tāni karmāṇi
nibadhnanti dhanañjaya
udāsīnavad-āsīnam
asaktaṁ teṣu karmasu

Nor do these works bind Me, O Dhananjaya, for I am seated above, as if indifferent, unattached to those actions.

Chapter 9, Verse 10

mayādhyakṣeṇa prakṛtiḥ
sūyate sacarācaram
hetunānena kaunteya
jagad viparivartate

I am the presiding control of My own Prakriti, not a spirit born in Her, but the creative spirit who causes Her to produce all that appears in the manifestation. Because of this, O Kaunteya, the world proceeds in cycles.

Chapter 9, Verse 11

avajānanti māṁ mūḍhā
mānuṣīṁ tanum-āśritam
paraṁ bhāvam ajānanto
mama bhūta-maheśvaram

Deluded minds disregard Me in this human body, because they know not My Supreme Nature as the Lord of all existences.

Chapter 9, Verse 12

moghāśā mogha-karmāṇo
mogha-jñānā vicetasaḥ
rākṣasīm-āsurīṁ caiva
prakṛtiṁ mohinīṁ śritāḥ

All their hope, action, and knowledge are vain things when judged by the Divine and eternal standard; they dwell in the rakshasic and asuric nature which deludes the will and the intelligence.

Chapter 9, Verse 13

mahātmān-astu māṁ pārtha
daivīṁ prakṛtim-āśritāḥ
bhajanty-ananya-manaso
jñātvā-bhūtādim-avyayam

But the great souls, O Arjuna, who share My Divine Nature, adore Me with a single mind, knowing Me to be the immutable source of beings.

Chapter 9, Verse 14

satataṁ kīrtayanto māṁ
yatantaśca dṛḍha-vratāḥ
namasyantaśca māṁ bhaktyā
nitya-yuktā upāsate

Always adoring Me, steadfast in spiritual endeavour, bowing down to Me with devotion, they worship Me ever in yoga.

Chapter 9, Verse 15

jñāna yajñena cāpyanye
yajanto mām-upāsate
ekatvena pṛthaktvena
bahudhā viśvato-mukham

Others also seek Me out by the sacrifice of knowledge and worship Me in My Oneness, in all separate beings and all My million, universal faces.

Chapter 9, Verse 16

ahaṁ kratur-ahaṁ yajñāḥ
svadhāham aham auṣadham
mantro'ham aham-evājyam
aham-agnir-ahaṁ hutam

I am the ritual action, I am the sacrifice, I am the food oblation, I am the fire-giving herb, I am the mantra, I am also the butter, I am the flame and I am the offering.

Chapter 9, Verse 17

pitāham-asya jagato
mātā dhātā pitāmahaḥ
vedyaṁ pavitram oṁkāra
ṛk sāma yajur eva ca

I am the Father of this world, the Mother, the Ordainer, the first Creator, the object of knowledge, the sacred syllable *OM* and also the *Rig*, *Sama* and *Yajur Vedas*.

Chapter 9, Verse 18

gatir-bhartā prabhuḥ sākṣī
nivāsaḥ śaraṇaṁ suhṛt
prabhavaḥ pralayaḥ sthānaṁ
nidhānaṁ bījam avyayam

I am the path, the upholder, the Master, the witness, the house and country, the refuge, the kind friend; I am the birth and status and destruction of apparent existence, I am the imperishable seed of all and their eternal resting-place.

Chapter 9, Verse 19

tapāmyaham ahaṁ varṣaṁ
nigṛhṇāmy utsṛjāmi ca
amṛtaṁ caiva mṛtyuśca
sadasac-cāham arjuna

I give heat, I withhold and send forth the rain; immortality and death, existent and non-existent am I, O Arjuna.

Chapter 9, Verse 20

traividya māṁ somapāḥ pūta-pāpā
yajñāir iṣṭvā svargatiṁ prārthayante
te puṇyam āsādya surendra-lokam
aśnanti divyān divi deva-bhogān

The knowers of the triple Veda, who drink the soma, purify themselves from sin, worshipping Me with sacrifice, pray of Me the way to heaven: ascending to the heavenly worlds by their righteousness, they enjoy the divine feasts of the demigods in paradise.

Chapter 9, Verse 21

te taṁ bhuktvā svarga-lokaṁ viśālaṁ
kṣīṇe puṇye marta-lokaṁ viśanti
evaṁ trayī-dharmam anuprapannā
gatāgataṁ kāmakāmā labhante

Having enjoyed the vast realm of Heaven, they return to the realm of mortals when their merit is exhausted. Thus, those who follow the Vedic rituals, but are motivated by desire, achieve only repeated birth and death.

Chapter 9, Verse 22

ananyāś-cintayanto māṁ
ye janāḥ paryupāsate
teṣāṁ nityābhiyuktānāṁ
yoga-kṣemaṁ vahāmyaham

To those men who worship Me making Me alone the whole object of their thought, to those constantly in yoga with Me, I take charge of their prosperity and welfare.

Chapter 9, Verse 23

ye'pyanya-devatā-bhaktā
yajante śraddhayānvitāḥ
te'pi mām-eva kaunteya
yajanty-avidhi-pūrvakam

Even those who, endowed with faith are devoted to other gods, they worship Me alone, O Kaunteya, in an indirect manner.

Chapter 9, Verse 24

ahaṁ hi sarva-yajñānāṁ
bhoktā ca prabhur-eva ca
na tu mām-abhijānanti
tattvenātaś-cyavanti te

It is I myself who am the enjoyer and the Lord of all sacrifices, but they do not recognise Me in My true Nature and hence they fall.

Chapter 9, Verse 25

yānti deva-vratā devān
pitṛn-yānti pitṛ-vratāḥ
bhūtāni yānti bhūtejyā
yānti madyājino'pi mām

They who worship the demigods go to the demigods; to the ancestors go the ancestor-worshippers; to elemental spirits go those who sacrifice to elemental spirits; but My worshippers come to Me.

Chapter 9, Verse 26

patraṁ puṣpaṁ phalaṁ toyaṁ
yo me bhaktyā prayacchati
tad-ahaṁ bhakty-upahṛtam
aśnāmi prayatātmanaḥ

He who offers to Me with devotion a leaf, a flower, a fruit, or water, that offering of love from the striving soul, is acceptable to Me.

Chapter 9, Verse 27

yat-karoṣi yad-aśnāsi
yaj-juhoṣi dadāsi yat
yat-tapasyasi kaunteya
tat-kuruṣva mad-arpaṇam

Whatever you do, whatever you enjoy, whatever you sacrifice, whatever you give, whatever energy of tapasya, whatever the soul's will or effort that you put forth, make it an offering unto Me.

Chapter 9, Verse 28

śubhāśubha phalair-evaṁ
mokṣyase karma-bandhanaiḥ
saṁnyāsa yoga-yuktātmā
vimukto mām-upaiṣyasi

Thus will you be liberated from good and evil results which constitute the bonds of action; with your soul in union with the Divine through renunciation, you will become free and attain Me.

Chapter 9, Verse 29

samo'haṁ sarva-bhūteṣu
na me dveṣyo'sti na priyaḥ
ye bhajanti tu māṁ bhaktyā
mayi te teṣu cāpyaham

I am equal in all existences, none are dear to Me, none are hated; yet those who turn to Me with love and devotion, they are in Me and I am also in them.

Chapter 9, Verse 30

api-cet sudurācāro
bhajate mām-ananyabhāk
sādhur-eva sa mantavyaḥ
samyag-vyavasito hi saḥ

If even the most sinful person worships Me with devotion to no other, he must be regarded as righteous, for he has rightly resolved.

Chapter 9, Verse 31

kṣipraṁ bhavati dharmātmā
śāśvacchāntiṁ nigacchati
kaunteya prati-jānīhi
na me bhaktaḥ praṇaśyati

Swiftly he becomes a soul of righteousness and obtains eternal peace. This is My word of promise, O Arjuna, that he who loves Me, shall not perish.

Chapter 9, Verse 32

māṁ hi pārtha vyapāśritya
ye'pi syuḥ pāpa-yonayaḥ
striyo vaiśyās-tathā śūdrāḥ
te'pi yānti parāṁ gatim

Those who take refuge with Me, O Paartha, though outcasts, born from wombs of sin, women, Vaishyas, even Shudras, they also attain to the highest goal.

Chapter 9, Verse 33

kiṁ punar-brāhmaṇāḥ puṇyā
bhaktā rājarṣayas-tathā
anityam asukhaṁ lokam
imaṁ prāpya bhajasva mām

How much easier it is then for holy brahmins and devoted king-sages! You who have come to this transient and unhappy world, love and turn to Me.

Chapter 9, Verse 34

manmanā bhāva mad-bhakto
mad-yājī māṁ namas-kuru
māmevaiṣyasi yuktvaivam
ātmānaṁ mat parāyaṇam

Focus your mind on Me, be devoted to Me, offer worship to Me, bow down to Me. Engaging your mind in this manner and regarding Me as the supreme goal, you will come to Me.

hariḥ oṁ tat sat
iti śrīmad bhagavad gītā sūpaniṣatsu
brahma vidyāyāṁ yoga
śāstre śrī kṛṣṇārjuna saṁvāde rājavidyā
rājaguhya yogaḥ nāma navamo 'dhyāyaḥ

Thus ends Chapter 9: Raajavidyaa Raajaguhya Yoga, from the dialogue between Sri Krishna and Arjuna in the *Upanishad* known as *Shreemad Bhagavad Gita*, the science of the Absolute, the yoga shastra.

CHAPTER 10
VIBHUTI YOGA

atha daśamo 'dhyāyaḥ

Here begins the tenth chapter

Chapter 10, Verse 1

śrī bhagavān uvāca
bhūya eva mahā-bāho
śṛṇu me paramaṁ vacaḥ
yatte'haṁ prīyamāṇāya
vakṣyāmi hita-kāmyayā

The Lord says: Again, O mighty-armed, hearken to My supreme words, that I will speak to you from My Will for your soul's good, now that your heart is taking delight in Me.

Chapter 10, Verse 2

na me viduḥ sura-gaṇāḥ
prabhavaṁ na maharṣayaḥ
aham-ādir-hi devānāṁ
maharṣīṇāṁ ca sarvaśaḥ

Neither the gods nor the great rishis know any birth of Me, for I am altogether and in every way the origin of the gods and the great rishis.

Chapter 10, Verse 3

yo mām ajam anādiṁ ca
vetti loka-maheśvaram
asamūḍhaḥ sa martyeṣu
sarva-pāpaiḥ pramucyate

One who knows Me as unborn and without a beginning; the great Lord of the worlds - is undeluded among mortals and is liberated from all negative acts.

Chapter 10, Verses 4-5

buddhir-jñānam asammohaḥ
kṣamā satyaṁ damaḥ śamaḥ
sukhaṁ duḥkhaṁ bhavo'bhāvo
bhayaṁ cābhayam eva ca

ahiṁsā samatā tuṣṭih
tapo dānaṁ yaśo'yaśaḥ
bhavanti bhāvā bhūtānāṁ
matta eva pṛthag-vidhāḥ

Intelligence, knowledge, non-delusion, forbearance, truth, restraint, self-control, pleasure and pain, exaltation and depression, fear and fearlessness, non-violence, equanimity, cheerfulness, austerity, beneficence, fame and infamy - these different qualities arise from Me alone.

Chapter 10, Verse 6

maharṣayaḥ sapta pūrve
catvāro manavas-tathā
mad-bhāvā mānasā jātā
yeṣāṁ loka imāḥ prajāḥ

The great Sapta-Rishis, the seven Ancients of the world, and before them the four other great sages, and also the four Manus, are My mental expansions. From them do all the living creatures in the world originate.

Chapter 10, Verse 7

etāṁ vibhūtiṁ yogaṁ ca
mama yo vetti tattvataḥ
so'vikalpena yogena
yujyate nātra saṁśayaḥ

Whosoever knows in truth, My Divine Glory and My Yoga, is united with the unswerving union: of this there is no doubt.

Chapter 10, Verse 8

ahaṁ sarvasya prabhavo
mattaḥ sarvaṁ pravartate
iti matvā-bhajante māṁ
budhā bhāva-samanvitāḥ

I am the birth of everything and from Me all proceeds into development of action and movement; understanding thus, the wise adore Me in complete devotion.

Chapter 10, Verse 9

mac-cittā mad-gata-prāṇā
bodhayantaḥ parasparam
kathayantaśca māṁ nityaṁ
tuṣyanti ca ramanti ca

Their consciousness full of Me, their life wholly given up to Me, illumining each other, mutually talking about Me, they are ever-contented and joyful.

Chapter 10, Verse 10

teṣāṁ satata-yuktānāṁ
bhajatāṁ prīti-pūrvakam
dadāmi buddhi-yogaṁ taṁ
yena mām-upayānti te

To these who are thus in a constant union with Me, and adore Me with an intense delight of Love, I give the Yoga of understanding by which they come to Me.

Chapter 10, Verse 11

teṣām evānukam pārtham
aham ajñānajaṁ tamaḥ
nāśayāmy-ātmabhāvastho
jñāna-dīpena-bhāsvatā

Out of compassion for them, I, lodged in their Self, lift the blazing lamp of knowledge and destroy the darkness which is born of ignorance.

Chapter 10, Verse 12

arjuna uvāca
paraṁ brahma paraṁ dhāma
pavitraṁ paramaṁ bhavān
puruṣaṁ śāśvataṁ divyam
ādidevam ajaṁ vibhum

Arjuna says: You are the Supreme Brahman, the Supreme Abode, the supreme purity, the One permanent, the Divine Purusha, Narayana Himself, the unborn, the all-pervading Lord.

Chapter 10, Verse 13

āhus tvām ṛṣayaḥ sarve
devārṣir-nāradas-tathā
asito devalo vyāsaḥ
svayaṁ caiva bravīṣi me

All the rishis say this of You and the divine seers Narada, Asita, Devala, Vyasa, and You Yourself say it to me.

Chapter 10, Verse 14

sarvam etad ṛtaṁ manye
yan-māṁ vadasi keśava
na hi te bhagavan vyaktiṁ
vidur-devā na dānavāḥ

All this that You say, my mind holds for the Truth, O Keshava. Neither the gods nor the demons, O blessed Lord, know Your manifestation.

Chapter 10, Verse 15

svayam evātmanātmānaṁ
vettha tvaṁ puruṣottama
bhūta-bhāvana bhūteśa
deva-deva jagat-pate

You alone know Yourself by Yourself, O Purushottama: Source of beings, Lord of beings, God of gods, Master of the universe!

Chapter 10, Verse 16

vaktum arhasy-aśeṣeṇa
divyā hyātma vibhūtayaḥ
yābhir-vibhūtibhir lokān
imāṁs tvaṁ vyāpya tiṣṭhasi

You should tell me of Your Divine Self-manifestations, all without exception. Your Vibhutis by which You stand pervading these worlds.

Chapter 10, Verse 17

katham vidyām ahaṁ yogiṁs
tvāṁ sadā paricintayan
keṣu keṣu ca bhāveṣu
cintyo'si bhagavan mayā

How shall I know You, O Yogi, by thinking of You everywhere at all moments and in what pre-eminent becomings should I think of You, O Lord?

Chapter 10, Verse 18

vistareṇātmano yogaṁ
vibhūtiṁ ca janārdana
bhūyaḥ kathaya tṛptir hi
śṛṇvato nāsti me'mṛtam

In detail tell me of Your Yoga and Vibhuti, O Janardana, tell me ever more of it; it is nectar of immortality to me, and however much of it I hear, I am not satisfied.

Chapter 10, Verse 19

śrī bhagavān uvāca
hanta te kathayiṣyāmi
divyā hyātma vibhūtayaḥ
prādhānyataḥ kuru-śreṣṭha
nāsty-anto vistarasya me

The Lord says: Yes, I will tell you of My Divine Vibhutis, but only in some of My principal pre-eminences, O best of the Kurus; for there is no end to the detail of My Self-extension in the universe.

Chapter 10, Verse 20

aham ātmā guḍākeśa
sarva bhūtāśaya sthitaḥ
aham ādiśca madhyaṁ ca
bhūtānām anta eva ca

I, O Arjuna, am the Self, which abides within all beings. I am the beginning and middle and end of all beings.

Chapter 10, Verse 21

ādityānām ahaṁ viṣṇur
jyotiṣāṁ ravir-aṁśumān
marīcir marutām asmi
nakṣatrāṇām ahaṁ śaśī

Among the Adityas, I am Vishnu; among lights and splendours, I am the radiant Sun; I am Marichi among the Maruts; among the stars, the Moon am I.

Chapter 10, Verse 22

vedānāṁ sāma-vedo'smi
devānām asmi vāsavaḥ
indriyāṇāṁ manaścāsmi
bhūtānām asmi cetanā

Among the *Vedas,* I am the *Sama Veda*; among the gods, I am Vasava; I am mind among the senses; in living beings, I am consciousness.

Chapter 10, Verse 23

rudrāṇāṁ śaṅkaraścāsmi
vitteśo yakṣa-rakṣasām
vasūnāṁ pāvakaścāsmi
meruḥ śikhariṇām aham

I am Shiva among the Rudras; the lord of wealth among the yakshas and rakshasas; Agni among the Vasus; Meru among the peaks of the world am I.

Chapter 10, Verse 24

purodhasāṁ ca mukhyaṁ māṁ
viddhi pārtha bṛhaspatim
senānīnām ahaṁ skandaḥ
sarasām asmi sāgaraḥ

And know Me, O Paartha, of the high priests of the world, the chief, Brihaspati; I am Skanda, the war-god, leader of the leaders of battle; among the flowing waters, I am the ocean.

Chapter 10, Verse 25

maharṣīṇāṁ bhṛgur ahaṁ
girām-asmy-ekam akṣaram
yajñānāṁ japa-yajño'smi
sthāvarāṇāṁ himālāyaḥ

I am Bhrigu among the great rishis; I am the sacred syllable *OM* among words; among acts of worship, I am Japa; among the mountain ranges, I am Himalaya.

Chapter 10, Verse 26

aśvatthaḥ sarva vṛkṣāṇāṁ
devārṣīṇāṁ ca nāradaḥ
gandharvāṇāṁ citrarathaḥ
siddhānāṁ kapilo muniḥ

I am the Ashwattha among all plants and trees; I am Narada among the divine sages; Chitraratha among the gandharvas; the Muni Kapila among the siddhas.

Chapter 10, Verse 27

uccaiḥśravasam aśvānāṁ
viddhi mām amṛtodbhavam
airāvataṁ gajendrāṇāṁ
narāṇāṁ ca narādhipam

Ucchaihshravas among horses, the nectar-born; Airavata among lordly elephants; and among men, the monarch.

Chapter 10, Verse 28

āyudhānām ahaṁ vajraṁ
dhenūnām asmi kāmadhuk
prajanaścāsmi kandarpaḥ
sarpāṇām asmi vāsukiḥ

Among weapons, I am the divine thunderbolt; I am Kamadhenu, the cow of plenty, among the cows; I am Kandarpa, the god of desire, among the progenitors; among the serpents, Vasuki am I.

Chapter 10, Verse 29

anantaścāsmi nāgānāṁ
varuṇo yādasām aham
pitṝṇām aryamā cāsmi
yamaḥ saṁyamatām aham

And I am Ananta among the nagas; Varuna among the peoples of the sea; Aryaman among the Fathers; Yamraj among those who maintain rule and law.

Chapter 10, Verse 30

prahlādaścāsmi daityānāṁ
kālaḥ kalayatām aham
mṛgāṇāṁ ca mṛgendro'haṁ
vainateyaśca pakṣiṇām

And I am Prahlad among the demons; I am Time, the head of all reckoning to those who reckon and measure; among the beasts of the forest, I am the lion; and Garuḍa, the son of Vinata, among birds.

Chapter 10, Verse 31

pavanaḥ pavatām asmi
rāmaḥ śastra-bhṛtām aham
jhaṣāṇāṁ makaraś-cāsmi
srotasām-asmi jāhnavī

I am the wind among purifiers; I am Rama among warriors; I am the shark among fish; among the rivers, Ganges am I.

Chapter 10, Verse 32

sargāṇām ādir-antaśca
madhyaṁ caivāham arjuna
adhyātma vidyā vidyānāṁ
vādaḥ pravadatām aham

Of creation I am the beginning and the end and also the middle, O Arjuna. I am spiritual knowledge among the many philosophies, arts and sciences; I am the logic of those who debate.

Chapter 10, Verse 33

akṣarāṇām akāro'smi
dvandvaḥ sāmāsikasya ca
aham evākṣayaḥ kālo
dhātā'haṁ viśvato mukhaḥ

I am the letter A among letters; the dual among compound words. I am imperishable Time; I am the Master and Ruler of all existences, whose faces are everywhere.

Chapter 10, Verse 34

mṛtyuḥ sarva-haraś-cāham
udbhavaśca bhaviṣyatām
kīrtiḥ śrīr-vāk ca nārīṇāṁ
smṛtir-medhā dhṛtiḥ kṣamā

I am all-snatching death, and I am too the originating cause of all that shall come into being. Among women, I am fame, grace, eloquence, presence of mind, intelligence, endurance, patience and forgiveness.

Chapter 10, Verse 35

bṛhatsāma tathā sāmnāṁ
gāyatrī chandasām aham
māsānāṁ mārgaśīrṣo'ham
ṛtūnāṁ kusumākaraḥ

Of the hymns in the *Sama Veda*, I am the *Brihat Sama*; of the metres, I am the Gayatri; of the months, I am Margasirsha, first of the months; and I am Spring, the fairest of seasons.

Chapter 10, Verse 36

dyūtaṁ chalayatām asmi
tejas tejasvinām aham
jayo'smi vyavasāyo'smi
sattvaṁ sattvavatām aham

I am the gambling of the cunning, and the strength of the mighty; I am resolution and perseverance and victory; I am the sattvic quality of the good.

Chapter 10, Verse 37

vṛṣṇīnāṁ vāsudevo'smi
pāṇḍavānāṁ dhanañjayaḥ
munīnām apy-ahaṁ vyāsaḥ
kavīnām uśanā kaviḥ

I am Krishna among the Vrishnis; Arjuna among the Pandavas; I am Vyasa among the sages; I am Ushana among the seers.

Chapter 10, Verse 38

daṇḍo damayatām asmi
nītir-asmi jigīṣatām
maunaṁ caivāsmi guhyānāṁ
jñānaṁ jñānavatām aham

I am the mastery and power of all who rule and tame and vanquish and the policy of all who succeed and conquer; I am the silence of things secret and the knowledge of the knower.

Chapter 10, Verse 39

yaccāpi sarva bhūtānāṁ
bījaṁ tad aham arjuna
na tadasti vinā yat syān
mayā bhūtaṁ carācaram

And whatsoever is the seed of all existences, that am I, O Arjuna; nothing moving or unmoving, animate or inanimate in the world can be without Me.

Chapter 10, Verse 40

nānto'sti mama divyānāṁ
vibhūtīnāṁ parantapa
eṣa tūddeśataḥ prokto
vibhūter vistaro mayā

There is no numbering or limit to My Divine Vibhutis, O Parantapa; what I have spoken, is nothing more than a summary development and I have given only the light of a few leading indications.

Chapter 10, Verse 41

yad yad vibhūtimat sattvaṁ
śrīmad ūrjitam eva vā
tat tad evāvagaccha tvaṁ
mama tejo'ṁśa saṁbhavam

Whatever exists that is beautiful, magnificent, glorious or powerful, know that all those manifestations arise from a fraction of My Divine Glory.

Chapter 10, Verse 42

athavā bahunaitena
kiṁ jñānena tavārjuna
viṣṭabhyāham-idaṁ kṛtsnam
ekāṁśena sthito jagat

But of what use to you is all this extensive knowledge, O Arjuna? I abide, sustaining this whole universe with but a fraction of Myself.

hariḥ oṁ tat sat
iti śrīmad bhagavad gītā sūpaniṣatsu
brahma vidyāyāṁ yoga śāstre śrīkṛṣṇārjuna
saṁvāde vibhūti yogaḥ nāma daśamo
'dhyāyaḥ

Thus ends Chapter 10: Vibhuti Yoga, from the dialogue between Sri Krishna and Arjuna in the *Upanishad* known as *Shreemad Bhagavad Gita*, the science of the Absolute, the yoga shastra.

CHAPTER 11
VISHWARUPA DARSHANA YOGA

atha ekādaśo 'dhyāyaḥ

Here begins the eleventh chapter

Chapter 11, Verse 1

arjuna uvāca
mad-anugrahāya paramaṁ
guhyam adhyātma saṁjñitam
yat tvayoktaṁ vacas tena
moho-yaṁ vigato mama

Arjuna says: This word of the highest spiritual secret of existence You have spoken out of compassion for me; by this my delusion is dispelled.

Chapter 11, Verse 2

bhavāpyayau hi bhūtānāṁ
śrutau vistaraśo mayā
tvattaḥ kamala-patrākṣa
māhātmyam api cāvyayam

The birth and passing away of existences have been heard by me in detail from You, O Lotus-eyed, and also the imperishable greatness of the Divine Supreme Self.

Chapter 11, Verse 3

evam etad yathāttha tvam
ātmānaṁ parameśvara
draṣṭum icchāmi te rūpam
aiśvaraṁ puruṣottama

So it is, as You have declared Yourself, O Supreme Lord; I desire to see Your Divine Form and Body, O Purushottama.

Chapter 11, Verse 4

manyase yadi tacchakyaṁ
mayā draṣṭum iti prabho
yogeśvara tato me tvaṁ
darśayāmānam avyayam

If You think that it can be seen by me, O Lord, O Master of Yoga, then show me Your imperishable Self.

Chapter 11, Verse 5

śrī bhagavān uvāca
paśya me pārtha rūpāṇi
śataśo'tha sahasraśaḥ
nānā vidhāni divyāni
nānā varṇā kṛtīni ca

The Lord says: Behold, O Paartha, my hundreds and thousands of divine forms, various in kind, various in shape and hue.

Chapter 11, Verse 6

paśyādityān vasūn rudrān
aśvinau marutas tathā
bahūny-adṛṣṭa-pūrvāṇi
paśyāścaryāṇi bhārata

Behold the Adityas, the Vasus, the Rudras, the two Ashwins and also the Maruts; behold many wonders that none has beheld, O Bharata.

Chapter 11, Verse 7

ihaikasthaṁ jagat kṛtsnaṁ
paśyādya sacarācaram
mama dehe gudākeśa
yac cānyad draṣṭum icchasi

Here, today, behold the whole world, with all that is moving and unmoving, unified in My body, O Arjuna, and whatever else you wish to see.

Chapter 11, Verse 8

na tu māṁ śakyase draṣṭum
anenaiva sva-cakṣuṣā
divyaṁ dadāmi te cakṣuḥ
paśya me yogam aiśvaram

This is a verse where the Lord reveals Himself to Arjuna: What you have to see, this your human eye cannot grasp; but there is a divine eye, an inmost seeing, and that eye I now give to you. Behold Me in My divine power.

Chapter 11, Verses 9-14

sañjaya uvāca
evam uktvā tato rāja
mahāyogeśvaro hariḥ
darśayāmāsa pārthāya
paramaṁ rūpam aiśvaram

aneka vaktra nayanam
anekādbhuta darśanam
aneka divyābharaṇaṁ
divyānekodyatāyudham

divya mālyāmbaradharaṁ
divya gandhānulepanam
sarvāścaryam ayaṁ devam
anantaṁ viśvato-mukham

divi sūrya sahasrasya
bhaved yugapad utthitā
yadi bhāḥ sadṛśī sā syād
bhāsas tasya mahātmanaḥ

tatraikasthaṁ jagat kṛtsnaṁ
pravibhaktam enekadhā
apaśyad deva-devasya
śarīre pāṇḍavas tadā

tataḥ sa vismayāviṣṭo
hṛṣṭa-romā dhanañjayaḥ
praṇamya śirasā devaṁ
kṛtāñjalir abhāṣata

Sanjaya says: Having thus spoken, O King, the Master of the great Yoga, Hari, showed to Paartha His Supreme Form. It is that of the infinite Supreme Lord whose faces are everywhere and in whom are all the wonders of existence, who multiplies unendingly all the many marvellous revelations of His being, a world-wide Divinity seeing with innumerable eyes, speaking from innumerable mouths, armed for battle with numberless divine uplifted weapons, glorious with divine ornaments of beauty, robed in heavenly raiment of deity, lovely with garlands of divine flowers, fragrant with divine perfumes. Such is the Light of this body of God as if a thousand suns had risen at once in Heaven. The whole world divided and yet unified is visible in the cosmic Body of the God of gods. Arjuna sees him and overcome with marvel and joy and fear he bows down and adores with words of awe and with clasped hands the tremendous vision.

Chapter 11, Verse 15

arjuna uvāca

paśyāmi devāṁs tava deva dehe
sarvāṁs tathā bhūta viśeṣa saṅghān
brahmāṇam īśaṁ kamalāsanastham
ṛṣīṁś ca sarvān uragāṁś ca divyān

Arjuna says: I see all the gods in Your body, O God, and different companies of beings, Brahma the creating Lord seated in the Lotus, and the Rishis and the race of the divine serpents.

Chapter 11, Verse 16

aneka bāhūdara vaktra netraṁ
paśyāmi tvāṁ sarvato'nanta rūpam
nāntaṁ na madhyaṁ na punastavādiṁ
paśyāmi viśveśvara viśvarūpa

I see numberless arms and bellies and eyes and faces, I see Your infinite forms on every side, but I see not Your end nor Your middle nor Your beginning, O Lord of the universe, O Form universal.

Chapter 11, Verse 17

kirīṭinaṁ gadinaṁ cakriṇaṁ ca
tejorāśiṁ sarvato dīptimantam
paśyāmi tvāṁ durnirīkṣyaṁ samantād
dīptānalārka-dyutim aprameyam

I see You crowned and with Your mace and Your discus, hard to discern because You are a luminous mass of energy on all sides of me, an encompassing blaze, a sun-bright firebright Immeasurable.

Chapter 11, Verse 18

tvam akṣaraṁ paramaṁ veditavyaṁ
tvam-asya viśvasya paraṁ nidhānam
tvam-avyayaḥ śāśvata dharma goptā
sanātanas tvaṁ puruṣo mato me

You are the Supreme Immutable whom we have to know, You are the high foundation and abode of the universe, You are the imperishable guardian of the eternal laws, You are the eternal soul of existence.

Chapter 11, Verse 19

anādi madhyāntam ananta-vīryam
ananta bāhuṁ śaśi-sūrya netram
paśyami tvāṁ dīpta hutāśa vaktraṁ
sva-tejasā viśvam idaṁ tapantam

I behold You without end or middle or beginning, of infinite force, of numberless arms, Your eyes are suns and moons, You have a face of blazing fire and You are ever burning up the whole universe with the flame of Your energy.

Chapter 11, Verse 20

dyāvāpṛthivyor idam antaraṁ hi
vyāptaṁ tvayaikena diśaśca sarvāḥ
dṛṣṭvādbhutaṁ rūpam ugraṁ tavedaṁ
loka trayaṁ pravyathitaṁ mahātman

The whole space between Earth and Heaven is occupied by You alone, when is seen this Your fierce and astounding Form, the three worlds are all in pain and suffer, O You mighty Spirit.

Chapter 11, Verse 21

amī hi tvāṁ surasaṅghā viśanti
kecid bhītāḥ prāñjalayo gṛṇanti
svastītyuktvā maharṣi siddha-saṅghāḥ
stuvanti tvāṁ stutibhiḥ puṣkalābhiḥ

Verily into You the hosts of devas enter. Some fearfully extol You with palms joined. The hosts of great sages and siddhas praise You with perfect eulogies saying, "Hail to You."

Chapter 11, Verse 22

rudrādityā vasavo ye ca sādhyā
viśve'śvinau marutaścoṣmapāśca
gandharva yakṣāsura siddha-saṅghā
vīkṣante tvāṁ vismitāścaiva sarve

The Rudras, Adityas, Vasus, Sadhyas, Vishvas, the two Aswins and the Maruts and the Ushmapas, the gandharvas, yakshas, asuras, siddhas, all have their eyes fixed on You in amazement.

Chapter 11, Verse 23

rūpaṁ mahatte bahu vaktra netraṁ
mahābāho bahu-bāhūru-pādam
bahūdaraṁ bahu daṁṣṭrā-karālaṁ
dṛṣṭvā lokāḥ pravyathitās tathāham

Beholding Your almighty manifestation with many faces and eyes with many arms, thighs, and feet, with many torsos and dreadful with many fangs, all beings including myself are terrified, O Krishna.

Chapter 11, Verse 24

nabhaḥ-spṛśaṁ dīptam aneka varṇaṁ
vyāttānanaṁ dīpta viśāla-netram
dṛṣṭvā hi tvāṁ pravyathitāntarātmā
dhṛtiṁ na vindāmi śamaṁ ca viṣṇo

I see You, touching heaven, blazing, of many hues, with opened mouths and enormous burning eyes, troubled and in pain is the soul within me and I find no peace or gladness.

Chapter 11, Verse 25

daṁṣṭrā-karālāni ca te mukhāni
dṛṣṭvaiva kālānala sannibhāni
diśo na jāne na labhe ca śarma
prasīda deveśa jagannivāsa

As I look upon Your mouths terrible with many tusks of destruction. Your faces like the fires of death and Time, I lose sense of the directions and find no peace. Turn Your heart to Grace, O God of gods! Refuge of all the worlds!

Chapter 11, Verses 26-27

amī ca tvāṁ dhṛtarāṣṭrasya putrāḥ
sarve sahaivāvanipāla saṅghaiḥ
bhīṣmo droṇaḥ sūta-putras tathāsau
sahāsmadīyairapi yodha-mukhyaiḥ

vaktrāṇi te tvaramāṇā viśanti
daṁṣṭrā-karālāni bhayānakāni
kecid vilagnā daśanāntareṣu
sandṛśyante cūrṇitair-uttamāṅgaiḥ

The sons of Dhritarashtra, all with the multitude of kings and heroes, Bhishma and Drona and Karna along with the foremost warriors on our side too, are hastening into Your tusked and terrible jaws and some are seen with crushed and bleeding heads caught between Your teeth of power.

Chapter 11, Verse 28

yathā nadīnāṁ bahavo'mbuvegāḥ
samudram evābhimukhā dravanti
tathā tavāmī naraloka vīrā
viśanti vaktrāṇy abhivijvalanti

As is the speed of many rushing waters racing towards the ocean, so all these heroes of the world of men are entering into Your many mouths of flame.

Chapter 11, Verse 29

yathā pradīptaṁ jvalanaṁ pataṅgā
viśanti nāśāya samṛddha-vegāḥ
tathaiva nāśāya viśanti lokās
tavāpi vaktrāṇi samṛddha-vegāḥ

As a swarm of moths with ever-increasing speed fall to their destruction into a fire that someone has kindled, so now are men with ever-increasing speed entering into Your jaws of doom.

Chapter 11, Verse 30

lelihyase grasamānaḥ samantāt
lokān samagrān vadanair jvaladbhiḥ
tejobhir āpūrya jagat samagraṁ
bhāsas tavogrāḥ pratapanti viṣṇoḥ

You lick the regions all around with Your tongues and You are swallowing up all the worlds in Your mouths of burning; all the universe is filled with the blaze of Your energies; fierce and terrible are Your lustres and they burn us, O Vishnu.

Chapter 11, Verse 31

ākhyāhi me ko bhavān-ugra-rūpo
namo'stu te deva-vara prasīda
vijñātum icchāmi bhavantam-ādyaṁ
na hi prajānāmi tava pravṛttim

O Fearsome One! Tell me who You are! Salutations to You, O Supreme God. Be gracious, I desire to know You, the Original One. I do not comprehend Your activity.

Chapter 11, Verse 32

śrī bhagavān uvāca
kālo'smi loka-kṣaya-kṛt pravṛddho
lokān samāhartum iha pravṛttaḥ
ṛte 'pi tvāṁ na bhaviṣyanti sarve
ye'vasthitāḥ pratyanīkeṣu yodhāḥ

The Lord says: I am Time, the mighty force which destroys everything, fully Manifesting Myself, I am here engaged in destroying the worlds. Even without you, none of the warriors arrayed in the enemy ranks shall survive.

Chapter 11, Verse 33

tasmāt tvam uttiṣṭha yaśo labhasva
jitvā śatrūn bhuṅkṣva rājyaṁ samṛddham
mayaivaite nihatāḥ pūrvam eva
nimitta-mātraṁ bhava savyasācin

Therefore, arise, win glory! Conquering your foes, enjoy a prosperous kingdom. They have verily already been slain by Me; act merely as an instrument, O Arjuna, you great Archer!

Chapter 11, Verse 34

droṇaṁ ca bhīṣmaṁ ca jayadrathaṁ ca
karṇaṁ tathā'nyānapi yodhavīrān
mayā hatāṁs-tvaṁ jahi mā vyathiṣṭhā
yudhyasva jetāsi raṇe sapatnān

Slay Drona, Bhishma, Jayadratha, Karna as well as other mighty warriors, who have been destroyed by Me. Do not vacillate, fight! You shall surely conquer your opponents in the battle.

Chapter 11, Verse 35

sañjaya uvāca
etacchrutvā vacanaṁ keśavasya
kṛtāñjalir vepamānaḥ kirīṭī
namaskṛtvā bhūya evāha kṛṣṇaṁ
sagadgadaṁ bhītabhītaḥ praṇamya

Sanjaya says: Having heard these words of Keshava, Arjuna, with clasped hands and trembling, saluted again and spoke to Krishna in a faltering voice, very much terrified and bowing down.

Chapter 11, Verse 36

arjuna uvāca
sthāne hṛṣīkeśa tava prakīrtyā
jagat prahṛṣyaty-anurajyate ca
rakṣāṁsi bhītāni diśo dravanti
sarve namasyanti ca siddha-saṅghāḥ

Arjuna says: Rightly and in good place, O Krishna, does the world rejoice and take pleasure in Your Name;

the rakshasas are fleeing from You in terror to all the quarters and the companies of the siddhas bow down before You in adoration.

Chapter 11, Verse 37

kasmācca te na nameran mahātman
garīyase brahmaṇo'pyādikartre
ananta deveśa jagan-nivāsa
tvam akṣaraṁ sadasat tatparaṁ yat

How should they not do You homage, O great Spirit? For You are the original Creator and Doer of works and greater even than creative Brahma. O You Infinite, O You God of gods, O You abode of the universe, You are the imperishable individual Self, the existent and the non-existent, and that which is beyond both.

Chapter 11, Verse 38

tvam ādidevaḥ puruṣaḥ purāṇash
tvam asya viśvasya paraṁ nidhānam
vettāsi vedyaṁ ca paraṁ ca dhāma
tvayā tataṁ viśvam ananta rūpa

You are the ancient Soul and the first and original Supreme Lord and the supreme resting-place of this all; You are the knower and that which is to be known and the highest status; O infinite in Form, by You was extended the universe.

Chapter 11, Verses 39-40

vāyur-yamo'gnir-varuṇaḥ
śaśāṅkaḥ prajāpatis-tvaṁ prapitā-mahaśca
namo namaste'stu sahasra-kṛtvaḥ
punaśca bhūyo'pi namo namaste

namaḥ purastād atha pṛṣṭhas-te
namo'stu te sarvata eva sarva
ananta-vīryāmita-vikramas-tvaṁ
sarvaṁ samāpnoṣi tato'si sarvaḥ

You are Yama and Vayu and Agni and Soma and Varuna and Prajapati, father of creatures, and the great-grandsire. Salutation to You a thousand times over and again and yet again salutation, in front and behind and from every side, for You are each and all that is. Infinite in might and immeasurable in strength of action You pervade all and are everyone.

Chapter 11, Verses 41-42

sakheti matvā prasabhaṁ yaduktaṁ
he kṛṣṇa he yādava he sakheti
ajānatā mahimānaṁ tavedaṁ
mayā pramādāt praṇayena vāpi

yaccāvahāsārtham asatkṛto 'si
vihāra śayyāsana bhojaneṣu
eko'thavāpy acyuta tat-samakṣaṁ
tat kṣāmaye tvām aham aprameyam

For whatsoever I have spoken to You in rash vehemence, thinking of You only as my human friend and companion, 'O Krishna, O Yadava, O Comrade,' not knowing this Your greatness, in negligent error or in love, and for whatsoever disrespect was shown by me to You in jest, at play, on the couch and the seat and in the banquet, alone or in Your presence, O faultless One, I pray forgiveness from You, the immeasurable.

Chapter 11, Verse 43

pitāsi lokasya carācarasya
tvam-asya pūjyaśca gurur garīyān
na tvat samo'sty abhyadhikaḥ kuto'nyo
lokatraye'py apratima-prabhāva

You are the Father of all this world of the moving and unmoving; You are one to be worshipped and the most solemn object of veneration. None is equal to You, how then another greater in all the three worlds, O incomparable in might?

Chapter 11, Verse 44

tasmāt praṇamya praṇidhāya kāyaṁ
prasādaye tvām aham īśam īdyam
piteva putrasya sakheva sakhyuḥ
priyaḥ priyāyārhasi deva sohum

Therefore, I bow down before You and prostrate my body and I demand Grace of You the adorable Lord. As a father to his son, as a friend to his friend and comrade, as one dear to him who he loves, so should You, O Supreme Lord, bear with me.

Chapter 11, Verse 45

adṛṣṭa-pūrvaṁ hṛṣito'smi dṛṣṭvā
bhayena ca pravyathitaṁ mano me
tadeva me darśaya deva rūpaṁ
prasīda deveśa jagannivāsa

I have seen what never was seen before and I rejoice, but my mind is troubled with fear. O Supreme Lord, show me that other form of Thine; turn Your heart to Grace, O You Lord of the Gods, O You abode of this universe.

Chapter 11, Verse 46

kirīṭinaṁ gadinaṁ cakra-hastam
icchāmi tvāṁ draṣṭum ahaṁ tathaiva
tenaiva rūpeṇa catur-bhujena
sahasra-bāho bhava viśvamūrte

I would see You even as before crowned and with Your mace and discus. Assume Your four-armed shape, O thousand-armed, O Form universal.

Chapter 11, Verse 47

śrī bhagavān uvāca
mayā prasannena tavārjunedaṁ
rūpaṁ paraṁ darśitam ātma yogāt
tejomayaṁ viśvam anantam ādyaṁ
yan me tvad anyena na dṛṣṭa-pūrvam

The Lord says: This that you now see by My favour, O Arjuna, is My supreme shape, My Form of luminous energy, the universal, the infinite, the original which none but you amongst men has yet seen. I have shown it by My Divine potency.

Chapter 11, Verse 48

na veda yajñādhyayanair na dānair
na ca kriyābhir-na tapobhir-ugraiḥ
evaṁ rūpaḥ śakya ahaṁ nṛloke
draṣṭuṁ tvadanyena kuru-pravīra

Neither by the study of *Vedas* and sacrifices, nor by gifts or ceremonial rites or severe austerities, can this Form of Mine be seen by any other than yourself, O foremost of Kurus.

Chapter 11, Verse 49

mā te vyathā mā ca vimūdha bhāvo
dṛṣṭvā rūpaṁ ghoram īdṛṅ-mamedam
vyapetabhīḥ prīta-manāḥ punas tvaṁ
tad eva me rūpam idaṁ prapaśya

You should envisage this tremendous vision without pain, without confusion of mind, without any sinking of the members. Cast away fear and let your heart rejoice, behold again this other form of Mine.

Chapter 11, Verse 50

sañjaya uvāca
ityarjunaṁ vāsudevas tathoktvā
svakaṁ rūpaṁ darśayāmāsa bhūyaḥ
āśvāsayāmāsa ca bhītam-eva
bhūtvā punaḥ saumya vapur mahātmā

Sanjaya says: Vasudeva, having thus spoken to Arjuna, again manifested His normal (Narayana) image; the Mahatma again assuming the desired form of Grace and Love and sweetness consoled the terrified one.

Chapter 11, Verse 51

arjuna uvāca
dṛṣṭvedaṁ mānuṣaṁ rūpaṁ
tava saumyaṁ janārdana
idānīm asmi saṁvṛttaḥ
sa cetāḥ prakṛtiṁ gataḥ

Arjuna says: Beholding again Your gentle human form, O Janardana, my heart is filled with delight and I am restored to my own nature.

Chapter 11, Verses 52-54

śrī bhagavān uvāca
sudurdarśam idaṁ rūpaṁ
dṛṣṭavān asi yan mama
devā apy asya rūpasya
nityam darśana-kāṅkṣaṇaḥ

nāhaṁ vedair na tapasā
na dānena na cejyayā
śakya evaṁ vidho draṣṭuṁ
dṛṣṭavān asi māṁ yathā

bhaktyā tv-ananyayā śakya
aham evaṁ-vidho 'rjuna
jñātuṁ draṣṭuṁ ca tattvena
praveṣṭuṁ ca parantapa

The Lord says: The greater Form that you have seen is only for the rare highest souls. The gods themselves ever desire to look upon it. Nor can I be seen as you have seen Me by *Veda* or austerities or gifts or sacrifice; it can be seen, known, and entered into only by that Bhakti which regards, adores and loves Me alone in all things.

Chapter 11, Verse 55

mat karma-kṛn mat-paramo
mad-bhaktaḥ saṅga-varjitaḥ
nivairaḥ sarva bhūteṣu
yaḥ sa māmeti pāṇḍava

Be a doer of My works, accept Me as the supreme being and object, become My bhakta, be free from attachment and without enmity to all existences; for such a man comes to Me, O Pandava.

hariḥ oṁ tatsat
iti śrīmad bhagavad gītā sūpaniṣatsu
brahma vidyāyāṁ yoga śāstre śrī kṛṣṇārjuna
saṁvāde viśvarūpa darśana yogaḥ nāma
ekādaśo 'dhyāyaḥ

Thus ends Chapter 11: Vishwarupa Darshana Yoga, from the dialogue between Sri Krishna and Arjuna in the *Upanishad* known as *Shreemad Bhagavad Gita*, the science of the Absolute, the yoga shastra.

CHAPTER 12
BHAKTI YOGA

atha dvādaśo 'dhyāyaḥ

Here begins the twelfth chapter

Chapter 12, Verse 1

arjuna uvāca
evaṁ satata-yuktā ye
bhaktās-tvāṁ paryupāsate
ye cāpyakṣaram-avyaktaṁ
teṣāṁ ke yoga-vittamāḥ

Arjuna says: Those devotees who thus by a constant union seek after You, and those who seek after the unmanifested, Immutable, which of these have the greater knowledge of yoga?

Chapter 12, Verse 2

śrī bhagavān uvāca
mayyāveśya mano ye māṁ
nitya-yuktā upāsate
śraddhayā parayopetās
te me yuktatamā matāḥ

The Lord says: Those who found their mind in Me and by constant union, possessed of a supreme faith, seek after Me, I hold to be the most perfectly in union of yoga.

Chapter 12, Verses 3-4

ye tvakṣaram-anirdeśyam
avyaktaṁ paryupāsate
sarvatragam-acintyaṁ ca
kūṭastham acalaṁ dhruvam

saṁniyam endriya-grāmaṁ
sarvatra sama-buddhayaḥ
te prāpnuvanti mām-eva
sarva-bhūta-hite-ratāḥ

But those who seek after the indefinable unmanifested, Immutable omnipresent, unthinkable, self-poised, immobile, constant, having subdued all their senses, unprejudiced, intent on the welfare of all beings – they too come to Me alone.

Chapter 12, Verse 5

kleśo'dhikataras-teṣāṁ
avyaktā-sakta-cetasām
avyaktā hi gatir-duḥkhaṁ
dehavadbhir-avyāpyate

The difficulty of those who devote themselves to the search of the unmanifested Brahman is greater; it is a thing to which embodied souls can only arrive by a constant mortification, a suffering of all the repressed members, a stern difficulty and anguish of the nature.

Chapter 12, Verses 6-7

ye tu sarvāṇi karmāṇi
mayi saṁnyasya mat-parāḥ
ananyenaiva yogena
māṁ dhyāyanta upāsate

teṣāṁ ahaṁ samuddhartā
mṛtyu-saṁsāra-sāgarāt
bhavāmi na cirāt-pārtha
mayyāveśita-cetasām

But those who giving up all their actions to Me, and wholly devoted to Me, worship meditating on Me with an unswerving yoga, those who fix on Me all their consciousness, O Paartha, speedily I deliver them out of the sea of death-bound existence.

Chapter 12, Verse 8

mayyeva mana ādhatsva
mayi buddhiṁ niveśaya
nivasiṣyasi mayyeva
ata ūrdhvaṁ na saṁśayaḥ

On Me repose all your mind and lodge all thy understanding in Me; doubt not that you shall dwell in Me above this mortal existence.

Chapter 12, Verse 9

atha cittaṁ samādhātuṁ
na śaknoṣi mayi sthiram
abhyāsa-yogena tato
mām-icchāptuṁ dhanañjaya

And if you are not able to keep the consciousness fixed steadily in Me, then by the yoga of practice seek after Me, O Arjuna.

Chapter 12, Verse 10

abhyāse'pyasamartho'si
mat-karma paramo bhava
mad-artham api karmāṇi
kurvan siddhim avāpsyasi

If you are unable even to seek by practice, then be it your supreme aim to do My work; doing all actions for My sake, you shall attain perfection.

Chapter 12, Verse 11

athaitad apyaśakto'si
kartuṁ mad-yogam āśritaḥ
sarva karma phala tyāgaṁ
tataḥ kuru yatātmavān

But if even this constant remembering of Me and lifting up of your works to Me is felt beyond your power, then renounce all fruit of action with the self-controlled.

Chapter 12, Verse 12

śreyo hi jñānam abhyāsāt
jñānād-dhyānaṁ viśiṣyate
dhyānāt karma phala tyāgas
tyāgāt-chāntir anantaram

Better indeed is knowledge than practice, than knowledge, meditation is better; than meditation, renunciation of the fruit of action is better, on renunciation follows peace.

Chapter 12, Verses 13-14

adveṣṭā sarva bhūtānāṁ
maitraḥ karuṇa eva ca
nir-mamo nir-ahaṅkāraḥ
sama duḥkha sukha kṣamī

santuṣṭaḥ satataṁ yogī
yatātmā dṛḍha-niścayaḥ
mayyarpita mano buddhiḥ
yo mad-bhaktaḥ sa me priyaḥ

He who has no egoism, no notion of 'I' or 'my', who has friendship and pity for all beings and hate for no living thing, who has a tranquil equality to pleasure and pain, and is patient and forgiving, he who has a desireless content, the steadfast control of self and the firm unshakable will and resolution of the yogi and a love and devotion which gives up the whole mind and reason to Me, he is dear to Me.

Chapter 12, Verse 15

yasmān no dvijate loko
lokān nodvijate ca yaḥ
harṣāmarṣabhayo-dvegaiḥ
mukto yaḥ sa ca me priyaḥ

He by whom the world is not afflicted or troubled, who also is not afflicted or troubled by the world, who is freed from the troubled agitated lower Nature and from its waves of joy and fear and anxiety and resentment, he is dear to Me.

Chapter 12, Verse 16

anapekṣaḥ śucir dakṣaḥ
udāsīno gatavyathaḥ
sarvārambha parityāgī
yo mad bhaktaḥ sa me priyaḥ

He who desires nothing, is pure, skilful in all actions, indifferent to whatever comes, not pained or afflicted by any result or happening, who has given up all initiative of mundane action, he, My devotee, is dear to Me.

Chapter 12, Verse 17

yo na hṛṣyati na dveṣṭi
na śocati na kāṅkṣati
śubhāśubha parityāgī
bhaktimān yaḥ sa me priyaḥ

He who neither desires the pleasant and rejoices at its touch, nor detests the unpleasant and sorrows, who has abolished the distinction between fortunate and unfortunate happenings, he is dear to Me.

Chapter 12, Verses 18-19

samaḥ śatrau ca mitre ca
tathā mānāpamānayoḥ
śītoṣṇa sukha duḥkheṣu
samaḥ saṅga vivarjitaḥ

tulya nindā stutir maunī
santuṣṭo yena kenacit
aniketaḥ sthira-matiḥ
bhaktimān me priyo naraḥ

Equal to friend and enemy, equal to honour and insult, pleasure and pain, praise and blame, grief and happiness, heat and cold, silent, content and well-satisfied with anything and everything, not attached to person or thing, place or home, firm in mind, that man is dear to Me.

Chapter 12, Verse 20

ye tu dharmyāmṛtam idaṁ
yathoktaṁ paryupāsate
śraddha-dhānāḥ mat-paramā
bhaktāste'tīva me priyāḥ

But exceedingly dear to Me are those devotees who make Me their one supreme aim and follow out with a perfect faith and exactitude the immortalising Dharma described in this teaching.

hariḥ oṁ tat sat
iti śrīmad bhagavad gītā sūpaniṣatsu
brahma vidyāyāṁ yoga śāstre śrī kṛṣṇārjuna

saṁvāde bhakti yogaḥ nāma dvādaśo 'dhyāyaḥ

Thus ends Chapter 12: Bhakti Yoga, from the dialogue between Sri Krishna and Arjuna in the *Upanishad* known as *Shreemad Bhagavad Gita*, the science of the Absolute, the yoga shastra.

CHAPTER 13
KSHETRAKSHETRAJNA VIBHAAGA YOGA

atha trayodaśo 'dhyāyaḥ

Here begins the thirteenth chapter

Chapter 13, Verse 1

arjuna uvāca
prakṛtiṁ puruṣaṁ caiva
kṣetraṁ kṣetrajñam eva ca
etad veditum icchāmi
jñānaṁ jñeyaṁ ca keśava

Arjuna says: O Keshava, I desire to learn about the spirit and about matter, about the Field, Kshetra (Prakriti) and its Knower, the soul (Purusha), Kshetrajna, about knowledge and the knower.

Chapter 13, Verse 2

śrī bhagavān uvāca
idaṁ śarīraṁ kaunteya
kṣetram ityabhidhīyate
etad yo vetti taṁ prāhuḥ
kṣetrajña iti tad vidaḥ

The Lord says: This body, O Arjuna, is called the Field (Kshetra). One who knows it is called the 'Knower of the Field' (Kshetrajna), by the enlightened ones.

Chapter 13, Verse 3

kṣetrajñaṁ cāpi māṁ viddhi
sarva kṣetreṣu bhārata
kṣetra kṣetrajñayor-jñānaṁ
yat tajjñānam mataṁ param

Understand Me as the Knower of the Field in all Fields, O Bharata; it is the knowledge at once of the Field and its Knower which is the real illumination and only wisdom.

Chapter 13, Verse 4

tat kṣetraṁ yacca yādṛk ca
yad vikāri yataśca yat
sa ca yo yat prabhāvaśca
tat samāsena me śṛṇu

What that Field is and what is its character, nature, source, deformations, and what it is and what are its Powers, hear that now briefly from Me.

Chapter 13, Verse 5

ṛṣibhir bahudhā gītaṁ
chandobhir vividhaiḥ pṛthak
brahma-sūtrapadaiścaiva
hetumadbhir viniścitaiḥ

It has been sung by the Rishis in many ways in various inspired verses, and also by the *Brahma Sutras* which give us the rational and philosophic analysis.

Chapter 13, Verse 6

mahā-bhūtāny-ahaṅkāro
buddhir-avyaktam eva ca
indriyāṇi daśaikaṁ ca
pañca cendriya gocarāḥ

The indiscriminate unmanifest Energy; the five elemental states of matter; the ten senses and the one mind, intelligence and ego; the five objects of the senses. This is the constitution of the kshetra.

Chapter 13, Verse 7

icchā dveṣaḥ sukhaṁ duḥkhaṁ
saṅghātaścetanā dhṛtiḥ
etat kṣetraṁ samāsena
savikāram udāhṛtam

Attraction, aversion, pleasure and pain - thus the component elements of the Field, which is the basis of consciousness, have been recounted along with its modifications.

Chapter 13, Verse 8

amānitvam adambhitvam
ahiṁsā kṣāntir ārjavam
ācāryopāsanaṁ śaucaṁ
sthairyam ātma-vinigrahaḥ

A total absence of worldly pride and arrogance, harmlessness, a candid soul, a tolerant, long-suffering and kind heart, purity of mind and body, tranquil firmness and steadfastness, self-control and a masterful government of the lower nature and the heart's worship given to the Teacher.

Chapter 13, Verses 9-10

indriyārtheṣu vairāgyam
anahaṅkāra eva ca
janma-mṛtyu-jarā-vyādhi
duḥkha doṣānudarśanam

asaktir anabhiṣvaṅgaḥ
putra-dāra-gṛhādiṣu
nityaṁ ca sama-cittatvam
iṣṭān-iṣṭopapattiṣu

A firm removal of the natural being's attraction to the objects of the senses, a radical freedom from egoism. Absence of clinging to the attachment and absorption of family and home, a keen perception of the defective nature of the ordinary life of physical man with its aimless and painful subjection to birth and death and disease and age, a constant equality to all pleasant or unpleasant happenings.

Chapter 13, Verses 11-12

mayi cānanya-yogena
bhaktir-avyabhicāriṇī
vivikta deśa-sevitvaṁ
aratir jana-saṁsadi

adhyātmajñāna nityatvaṁ
tattva-jñānārtha darśanam
etajjñānam iti proktam
ajñānaṁ yadato'nyathā

A meditative mind turned towards solitude and away from the vain noise of crowds and the assemblies of men, a philosophic perception of the true sense and large principles of existence, a tranquil continuity of inner spiritual knowledge and light, the yoga of an unswerving devotion, Love of God, the heart's deep and constant adoration of the universal and eternal Presence. That is declared to be the knowledge; all against it is ignorance.

Chapter 13, Verse 13

jñeyaṁ yattat pravakṣyāmi
yajjñātvāmṛtam aśnute
anādi mat-paraṁ brahma
na sattannāsad ucyate

I shall declare that which has to be known, knowing which, one attains immortality - It is beginningless Brahman, to which I am superior; it is said to be neither being *(Sat)* nor non-being *(Asat)*.

Chapter 13, Verse 14

sarvataḥ pāṇi-pādaṁ tat
sarvato 'kṣi-śiro-mukham
sarvataḥ śṛutimalloke
sarvam-āvṛtya tiṣṭhati

His hands and Feet are on every side of us, His heads and eyes and faces are those innumerable visages which we see wherever we turn, His ear is everywhere, He immeasurably fills and surrounds all this world with Himself, He is the universal Being in whose embrace we live.

Chapter 13, Verse 15

sarvendriya guṇābhāsaṁ
sarvendriya vivarjitam
asaktaṁ sarva bhṛccaiva
nirguṇaṁ guṇabhoktṛ ca

All the senses and their qualities reflect Him but He is without any senses; He is unattached, yet all-supporting; He is enjoyer of the gunas, though not limited by them.

Chapter 13, Verse 16

bahir-antaśca bhūtānām
acaraṁ caram eva ca
sūkṣmatvāt tad avijñeyaṁ
dūrasthaṁ cāntike ca tat

That which is in us is He and all that we experience outside ourselves is He. The inward and the outward, the far and the near, the moving and the unmoving, all this He is at once. He is the subtlety of the subtle which is beyond our knowledge.

Chapter 13, Verse 17

avibhaktaṁ ca bhūteṣu
vibhaktam iva ca sthitam
bhūtabhartṛ ca tajjñeyaṁ
grasiṣṇu prabhaviṣṇu ca

Undivided and yet existing as if divided among beings, this Atma is to be known as the supporter of elements. It consumes and regenerates.

Chapter 13, Verse 18

jyotiṣām api tajjyotis
tamasaḥ param-ucyate
jñānaṁ jñeyaṁ jñāna-gamyaṁ
hṛdi sarvasya viṣṭhitam

He is the Light of all lights and luminous beyond all the darkness of our ignorance. He is knowledge and the object of knowledge. He is seated in the hearts of all.

Chapter 13, Verse 19

iti kṣetraṁ tathā jñānaṁ
jñeyaṁ coktaṁ samāsataḥ
mad bhakta etad vijñāya
mad bhāvāyopapadyate

Thus the Field, knowledge and the object of knowledge, have been briefly told. My devotee, thus knowing, attains to My status of Being.

Chapter 13, Verse 20

prakṛtiṁ puruṣaṁ caiva
viddhyānādī ubhāvapi
vikārāṁśca guṇāṁścaiva
viddhi prakṛti saṁbhavān

Know that Purusha (the soul) and Prakriti (nature) are both without origin and eternal; but the modes of nature and the lower forms She assumes to our conscious experience have an origin in Prakriti.

Chapter 13, Verse 21

kārya kāraṇa kartṛtve
hetuḥ prakṛtir ucyate
puruṣaḥ sukha-duḥkhānāṁ
bhoktṛtve hetur ucyate

The chain of cause and effect and the state of being the doer are created by Prakriti; Purusha enjoys pleasure and pain.

Chapter 13, Verse 22

puruṣaḥ prakṛtistho hi
bhuṅkte prakṛtijān guṇān
kāraṇaṁ guṇa-saṅgo 'sya
sadasad yoni janmasu

Purusha involved in Prakriti enjoys the qualities born of Prakriti; attachment to the gunas is the cause of birth in good and evil wombs.

Chapter 13, Verse 23

upadṛṣṭānumantā ca
bhartā bhoktā maheśvaraḥ
paramātmeti cāpyukto
deho'smin puruṣaḥ paraḥ

The embodied Self is called the witness, the sanctioner, supporter, experiencer, the great Lord and likewise the Supreme Purusha.

Chapter 13, Verse 24

ya evaṁ vetti puruṣaṁ
prakṛtiṁ ca guṇaiḥ saha
sarvathā vartamāno 'pi
na sa bhūyo 'bhijāyate

He who thus knows Purusha and Prakriti with Her qualities, howsoever he lives and acts, he shall not be born again.

Chapter 13, Verse 25

dhyānenātmani paśyanti
kecid ātmānam ātmanā
anye sāṅkhyena yogena
karma-yogena cāpare

This knowledge comes by an inner meditation through which the eternal Self becomes apparent to us in our self-existence. Or it comes by the yoga of the sankhyas (the separation of the soul from nature), or it comes by Karma Yoga.

Chapter 13, Verse 26

anye tvevam ajānantaḥ
śrutvānyebhya upāsate
te'pi cātitarantyeva
mṛtyuṁ śruti parāyaṇāḥ

Others, who are ignorant of these paths of yoga, may hear of the Truth from others and mould the mind into the sense of that to which it listens with faith and concentration. But however arrived at, it carries us beyond death to immortality.

Chapter 13, Verse 27

yāvat sañjāyate kiñcit
sattvaṁ sthāvara jaṅgamam
kṣetra kṣetrajña saṁyogāt
tad viddhi bharatarṣabha

Whatever being, moving or unmoving, is born, know, O best of the Bharatas, that it is from the union between the Field and the Knower of the Field.

Chapter 13, Verse 28

samaṁ sarveṣu bhūteṣu
tiṣṭhantaṁ parameśvaram
vinaśyatsv-avinaśyantaṁ
yaḥ paśyati sa paśyati

Seated equally in all beings, the Supreme Lord, unperishing within the perishing - he who thus sees, he sees.

Chapter 13, Verse 29

samaṁ paśyan hi sarvatra
samavasthitam īśvaram
na hinasty-ātmanātmānam
tato yāti parāṁ gatim

Perceiving the equal Lord as the spiritual inhabitant in all forces, in all things and in all beings, he does not injure himself by casting his being into the hands of desire and passions, and thus he attains to the supreme status.

Chapter 13, Verse 30

prakṛtyaiva ca karmāṇi
kriyamāṇāni sarvaśaḥ
yaḥ paśyati tathātmānam
akartāraṁ sa paśyati

He who sees that all action is verily done by Prakriti, and that the Self is the inactive witness, he sees reality.

Chapter 13, Verse 31

yadā bhūta pṛthag bhāvam
ekastham anupaśyati
tata eva ca vistāram
brahma saṁpadyate tadā

When he perceives the diversified existence of beings abiding in the one eternal Being, and spreading forth from it, then he attains to Brahman.

Chapter 13, Verse 32

anāditvān nirguṇatvāt
paramātmāyam avyayaḥ
śarīrastho'pi kaunteya
na karoti na lipyate

Because it is without origin and eternal, not limited by the qualities, the imperishable Supreme Self, though seated in the body, O Kaunteya, does not act, nor is affected.

Chapter 13, Verse 33

yathā sarvagataṁ saukṣmyād
ākāśaṁ nopalipyate
sarvatrāvasthito dehe
tathātmā nopalipyate

As the all-pervading ether is not affected by reason of its subtlety, so seated everywhere in the body, the Self is not affected.

Chapter 13, Verse 34

yathā prakāśayatyekaḥ
kṛtsnaṁ lokam imaṁ raviḥ
kṣetraṁ kṣetrī tathā kṛtsnaṁ
prakāśayati bhārata

As the one Sun illumines the entire Earth, so the Lord of the Field (Kshetrajna) illumines the entire Field, O Bharata.

Chapter 13, Verse 35

kṣetra kṣetrajñayor-evam
antaraṁ jñāna-cakṣuṣā
bhūta prakṛti-mokṣaṁ ca
ye vidur-yānti te param

They, who, with the eye of knowledge, perceive this difference between the Field and the Knower of the Field and the liberation of beings from Prakriti, attain to the Supreme.

hariḥ oṁ tat sat
iti śrīmad bhagavad gītā sūpaniṣatsu
brahma vidyāyāṁ yoga śāstre śrī kṛṣṇārjuna
saṁvāde kṣetrakṣetrajña vibhāga yogaḥ
nāma trayodaśo 'dhyāyaḥ

Thus ends Chapter 13: Kshetrakshetrajna Vibhaaga Yoga, from the dialogue between Sri Krishna and Arjuna in the *Upanishad* known as *Shreemad Bhagavad Gita*, the science of the Absolute, the yoga shastra.

CHAPTER 14
GUNATRAYA VIBHAAGA YOGA

atha caturdaśo 'dhyāyaḥ

Here begins the fourteenth chapter

Chapter 14, Verse 1

śrī bhagavān uvāca
paraṁ bhūyaḥ pravakṣyāmi
jñānānāṁ jñānam uttamam
yaj-jñātvā munayaḥ sarve
parāṁ siddhim ito gatāḥ

The Lord says: I will again declare the supreme knowledge, the highest of all knowings, which having known, all the sages have gone hence to the highest perfection.

Chapter 14, Verse 2

idaṁ jñānam upāśritya
mama sādharmyam āgatāḥ
sarge'pi nopajāyante
pralaye na vyathanti ca

Having taken refuge in this knowledge and become of like nature and law of being with Me, they are not born in the creation, nor troubled by the anguish of the universal dissolution.

Chapter 14, Verse 3

mama yonir mahad-brahma
tasmin garbham dadhāmyaham
saṁbhavaḥ sarva bhūtānāṁ
tato bhavati bhārata

My womb is the Mahat Brahman. Into that I cast the seed and thence spring all beings, O Bharata.

Chapter 14, Verse 4

sarva yoniṣu kaunteya
mūrtayaḥ sambhavanti yāḥ
tāsāṁ brahma mahad-yonir
ahaṁ bīja-pradaḥ pitā

Whatever forms are produced in whatsoever wombs, O Kaunteya, the Mahat Brahman is their womb, and I am the Father who casts the seed.

Chapter 14, Verse 5

sattvaṁ-rajas-tama iti
guṇāḥ prakṛti saṁbhavāḥ
nibadhnanti mahābāho
dehe dehinam avyayam

Sattva, rajas and tamas are the gunas that arise from Prakrti. They cause the bondage of the immutable Self to the body, O Arjuna.

Chapter 14, Verse 6

tatra sattvaṁ nirmalatvāt
prakāśakam anāmayam
sukha-saṅgena badhnāti
jñāna-saṅgena cānagha

Of these sattva is by the purity of its quality a cause of light and illumination, and by virtue of that purity produces no disease or morbidity or suffering in the nature: it binds by attachment to knowledge and attachment to happiness, O sinless one.

Chapter 14, Verse 7

rajo rāgātmakaṁ viddhi
tṛṣṇā-saṅga samudbhavam
tan nibadhnāti kaunteya
karma-saṅgena dehinam

Rajas has for its essence attraction of liking and longing; it is a child of the attachment of the soul to the desire of objects. O Kaunteya, it binds the embodied spirit by attachment to works.

Chapter 14, Verse 8

tamas tvajñānajaṁ viddhi
mohanaṁ sarva dehinām
pramād-ālasya nidrābhiḥ
tan nibadhnāti bhārata

But tamas, born of ignorance, is the deluded of all embodied beings; it binds by negligence, indolence and sleep, O Bharata.

Chapter 14, Verse 9

sattvaṁ sukhe sañjayati
rajaḥ karmaṇi bhārata
jñānam āvṛtya tu tamaḥ
pramāde sañjayaty-uta

Sattva attaches to happiness, rajas to action, O Bharata; tamas covers up the knowledge and attaches to negligence of error and inaction.

Chapter 14, Verse 10

rajas tamaścābhibhūya
sattvaṁ bhavati bhārata
rajah sattvaṁ tamaścaiva
tamah sattvaṁ rajastathā

Prevailing over rajas and tamas, sattva prevails, O Arjuna. Overwhelming tamas and sattva, rajas preponderates; overwhelming rajas and sattva, tamas predominates.

Chapter 14, Verse 11

sarva dvāreṣu dehe'smin
prakāśa upajāyate
jñānaṁ yadā tadā vidyād
vivṛddhaṁ sattvam ityuta

When into all the doors in the body there comes a flooding of Light, a Light of understanding, perception and knowledge, one should understand that there has been a great increase and uprising of the sattvic guna in the nature.

Chapter 14, Verse 12

lobhaḥ pravṛttir ārambhaḥ
karmaṇām aśamaḥ spṛhā
rajasyetāni jāyante
vivṛddhe bharatarṣabha

Greed, seeking impulsions, initiative of actions, unrest, desire - all this mounts in us when rajas increases.

Chapter 14, Verse 13

aprakāśo'pravṛttiśca
pramādo moha eva ca
tamasyetāni jāyante
vivṛddhe kuru-nandana

Nescience, inertia, negligence and delusion - these are born when tamas predominates, O joy of the Kurus.

Chapter 14, Verse 14

yadā sattve pravṛddhe tu
pralayaṁ yāti deha-bhṛt
tadottama vidāṁ lokān
amalān pratipadyate

If sattva prevails when the embodied goes to dissolution, then he attains to the spotless worlds of the knowers of the highest principles.

Chapter 14, Verse 15

rajasi pralayaṁ gatvā
karma saṅgiṣu jāyate
tathā pralīnas tamasi
mūdha-yoniṣu jāyate

Going to dissolution when rajas prevails, he is born among those attached to action; if dissolved during the increase of tamas, he is born in the wombs of beings involved in ignorance.

Chapter 14, Verse 16

karmaṇaḥ sukṛtasyāhuḥ
sāttvikaṁ nirmalaṁ phalam
rajas-astu phalaṁ duḥkham
ajñānaṁ tamasaḥ phalam

It is said the fruit of works rightly done is pure and sattvic; pain is the consequence of rajasic works, ignorance is the result of tamasic action.

Chapter 14, Verse 17

sattvāt sañjāyate jñānaṁ
rajaso lobha eva ca
pramāda-mohau tamaso
bhavato'jñānam eva ca

From sattva, knowledge is born, and greed from rajas; negligence and delusion are of tamas, and also ignorance.

Chapter 14, Verse 18

**ūrdhvaṁ gacchanti sattvasthā
madhye tiṣṭhanti rājasāḥ
jaghanya guṇa vṛttisthā
adho gacchanti tāmasāḥ**

They rise upwards who are in sattva; those in rajas remain in the middle; the tamasic, those enveloped in ignorance and inertia, the effect of the lowest quality, go downwards.

Chapter 14, Verse 19

**nānyaṁ guṇebhyaḥ kartāraṁ
yadā draṣṭānupaśyati
guṇebhyaśca paraṁ vetti
madbhāvaṁ so'dhigacchati**

When the seer perceives that the modes of nature are the whole agency and cause of works and knows and turns to That which is supreme above the gunas, he attains to Maha Bhav, the movement and status of the Divine.

Chapter 14, Verse 20

**guṇān etān atītya trīn
dehī deha samudbhavān
janma mṛtyu jarā duḥkhair
vimukto'mṛtam aśnute**

When the soul thus rises above the three gunas born of the embodiment in nature, he is freed from subjection to birth and death and their associates (decay, old age and suffering) and enjoys in the end the Immortality of its self-existence.

Chapter 14, Verse 21

arjuna uvāca

kair-liṅgais trīn guṇān etān
atīto bhavati prabho
kim ācāraḥ kathaṁ caitāṁs
trīn guṇān ativartate

Arjuna says: What are the signs of the man who has risen above the three gunas, O Lord? What is his action and how does he surmount the gunas?

Chapter 14, Verse 22

śrī bhagavān uvāca

prakāśaṁ ca pravṛttiṁ ca
moham-eva ca pāṇḍava
na dveṣṭi saṁpravṛttāni
na nivṛttāni kāṅkṣati

The Lord says: He, O Pandava, who does not detest or shrink from the operation of Enlightenment (the result of rising sattva) or impulsion to works (the result of rising rajas) or the clouding over of the mental and nervous being (the result of rising tamas), nor longs after them, when they cease.

Chapter 14, Verse 23

udāsīnavad āsīno
guṇair yo na vicālyate
guṇā vartanta ityeva
yo'vatiṣṭhati neṅgate

He who, established in a position as of one seated high above, is unshaken by the gunas; who seeing that it is the gunas that are in process of action stands apart immovable.

Chapter 14, Verses 24-25

sama duḥkha sukhaḥ svasthaḥ
sama loṣṭāśma kāñcanaḥ
tulya priyāpriyo dhīrah
tulya nindātma saṁstutiḥ

mānāpamānayos tulyas
tulyo mitrāri pakṣayoḥ
sarvārambha parityāgī
guṇātītaḥ sa ucyate

He who regards happiness and suffering alike, gold and mud and stone as of equal value, to whom the pleasant and the unpleasant, praise and blame, honour and insult, the faction of his friends and the faction of his enemies are equal things; who is steadfast in a wise imperturbable and immutable inner calm and quietude; who initiates no action but leaves all works to be done by the gunas of nature - he is said to be above the gunas.

Chapter 14, Verse 26

māṁ ca yo'vyabhicāreṇa
bhakti yogena sevate
sa guṇān samatītyaitān
brahma-bhūyāya kalpate

He also who loves and strives after Me with an undeviating love and adoration, passes beyond the three gunas and he too is prepared for becoming the Brahman.

Chapter 14, Verse 27

brahmaṇo hi pratiṣṭhā'ham
amṛtasyāvyayasya ca
śāśvatasya ca dharmasya
sukhasyaikāntikasya ca

I am the foundation of the silent Brahman and of immortality and imperishable spiritual existence and of the eternal dharma and of an utter bliss of happiness.

hariḥ oṁ tat sat
iti śrīmad bhagavad gītā sūpaniṣatsu
brahma vidyāyāṁ yoga śāstre śrī kṛṣṇārjuna
saṁvāde guṇatraya vibhāga yogaḥ nāma
caturdaśo 'dhyāyaḥ

Thus ends Chapter 14: Gunatraya Vibhaaga Yoga, from the dialogue between Sri Krishna and Arjuna in the *Upanishad* known as *Shreemad Bhagavad Gita*, the science of the Absolute, the yoga shastra.

CHAPTER 15
PURUSHOTTAMA YOGA

atha pañcadaśo 'dhyāyaḥ

Here begins the fifteenth chapter

Chapter 15, Verse 1

śrī bhagavān uvāca
ūrdhva mūlam adhaḥ śākham
aśvatthaṁ prāhur-avyayam
chandāṁsi yasya parṇāni
yastaṁ veda sa vedavit

The Lord says: With its original source above in the Eternal, its branches stretching below, the Ashwattha is said to be eternal and imperishable; the leaves of it are the hymns of the Veda; he who knows it is the Veda-knower.

Chapter 15, Verse 2

adhaścordhvaṁ prasṛtās tasya śākhā
gurapravṛddhā viṣaya pravālāḥ
adhaśca mūlāny-anusantatāni
karmānubandhīni manuṣya-loke

The branches of this cosmic tree extend both below and above, and they grow by the gunas of nature. The objects of the senses are its foliage, downward here into the world of men it plunges its roots of attachment and desire with their consequences of an endlessly developing action.

Chapter 15, Verses 3-4

na rūpam asyeha tathopalabhyate
nānto na cādir na ca saṁpratiṣṭhā
aśvattham enaṁ suvirūḍha-mūlam
asaṅga śastreṇa dṛḍheṇa chittvā

tataḥ padaṁ tat parimārgitavyaṁ
yasmin gatā na nivartanti bhūyaḥ
tameva cādyaṁ puruṣaṁ prapadye
yataḥ pravṛttiḥ prasṛtā purāṇī

The real form of it cannot be perceived by us in this material world of man's embodiment, nor its beginning nor its end, nor its foundation. Having cut down this firmly rooted Ashwattha by the strong sword of detachment, one should seek for that highest goal whence, once reached, there is no compulsion of return to mortal life. I turn away to seek that original Purusha alone from whom proceeds the ancient eternal urge to action.

Chapter 15, Verse 5

nirmāna mohā jita saṅga doṣā
adhyātma nityā vinivṛtta kāmāḥ
dvandvair vimuktāḥ sukha-duḥkha saṁjñaiḥ
gacchanty-amūḍhāḥ padam-avyayam tat

To be free from the bewilderment of this lower Maya - Apara Prakriti - without egoism, the great fault of attachment conquered, all desires stilled, the duality of joy and grief cast away, always to be fixed in a pure spiritual Consciousness, these are the steps of the way to the Supreme Infinite.

Chapter 15, Verse 6

na tad bhāsayate sūryo
na śaśāṅko na pāvakaḥ
yad gatvā na nivartante
taddhāma paramaṁ mama

There we find the timeless being which is not illumined by the Sun or the Moon or fire; having gone thither they do not return; that is the highest eternal status of My Being.

Chapter 15, Verse 7

mamaivāṁśo jīva-loke
jīva-bhūtas sanātanaḥ
manaṣ ṣaṣṭhān-īndriyāṇi
prakṛtisthāni karṣati

It is an eternal portion of Me that becomes the Jiva in the world of living creatures and cultivates the subjective powers of Prakriti, mind and the five senses.

Chapter 15, Verse 8

śarīraṁ yad avāpnoti
yaccāpy-utkrāmat-īśvaraḥ
gṛhītvaitāni saṁyāti
vāyur-gandhān ivāśayāt

Whatever body the ruler (Jivatma) acquires and from whatever body it departs, it proceeds, taking with it these sense-faculties just as the wind carries fragrance from their places in flowers.

Chapter 15, Verse 9

śrotraṁ cakṣuḥ sparśanaṁ ca
rasanaṁ ghrāṇam eva ca
adhiṣṭhāya manaścāyaṁ
viṣayān upasevate

The ear, the eye, the touch, the taste and the smell, using these and the mind also, he enjoys the objects of mind and senses, as the in-dwelling and over-dwelling Soul.

Chapter 15, Verse 10

utkrāmantaṁ sthitaṁ vāpi
bhuñjānaṁ vā guṇān-vitam
vimūḍhā nānupaśyanti
paśyanti jñāna-cakṣuṣaḥ

The deluded do not perceive it (the Jivatma) conjoined with the gunas when departing or staying or experiencing - only the enlightened ones see.

Chapter 15, Verse 11

yatanto yoginaścainaṁ
paśyanty-ātmany-avasthitam
yatanto'pyakṛtātmāno
nainaṁ paśyantyacetasaḥ

The yogis who strive, see the Lord in themselves; but though they strive to do so, the ignorant perceive Him not, as they are not formed in the spiritual mould.

Chapter 15, Verse 12

yadādityagataṁ tejo
jagad bhāsayate'khilam
yaccandramasi yaccāgnau
tat tejo viddhi māmakam

The light of the Sun that illumines all this world, that which is in the Moon and in fire, know that light to be Mine.

Chapter 15, Verse 13

gām āviśya ca bhūtāni
dhārayāmy-aham ojasā
puṣṇāmi cauṣadhīḥ sarvāḥ
somo bhūtvā rasātmakaḥ

And pervading the Earth I support all beings by My power. I nourish all herbs by becoming the Moon full of nectar.

Chapter 15, Verse 14

ahaṁ vaiśvānaro bhūtvā
prāṇināṁ deham āśritaḥ
prāṇāpāna samāyuktaḥ
pacāmyannaṁ caturvidham

I, having become the flame of life, sustain the physical body of living creatures, and united with Prana and Apana, digest the four kinds of food.

Chapter 15, Verse 15

sarvasya cāhaṁ hṛdi sanniviṣṭo
mattaḥ smṛtir jñānam apohanaṁ ca
vedaiśca sarvair aham eva vedyo
vedānta-kṛd vedavid eva cāham

And I am located in the hearts of all. From Me comes memory, knowledge and their absence also. Indeed, I alone am that which is to be known from all the *Vedas*. I bring about the fruition of the rituals of the *Vedas*; I alone am the knower of the *Vedas*.

Chapter 15, Verse 16

dvāvimau puruṣau loke
kṣaraś cākṣara eva ca
kṣaraḥ sarvāṇi bhūtāni
kūṭastho'kṣara ucyate

There are two Purushas (spiritual beings) in this world, the immutable and the mutable; the mutable is all these existences (Kshara), the Kutastha is called the immutable (Akshara).

Chapter 15, Verse 17

uttamaḥ puruṣas-tvanyaḥ
paramātmety-udāhṛtaḥ
yo loka-trayam-āviśya
bibharty-avyaya īśvaraḥ

Distinct from these (Kshara and Akshara) is the Supreme Person, described as the Supreme Self in the *Vedas*, He who, pervading the threefold universe, supports it as the Immutable One and the Lord.

Chapter 15, Verse18

yasmāt-kṣaram-atīto'ham
akṣarād-api cottamaḥ
ato'smi loke vede ca
prathitaḥ puruṣottamaḥ

Because I transcend the perishable and am also higher than the imperishable, I am declared to be the Supreme Being (Purushottama) in the smritis and the *Vedas*.

Chapter 15, Verse 19

yo mām-evam asammūḍho
jānāti puruṣottamam
sa sarva-vid bhajati māṁ
sarva bhāvena bhārata

He who undeluded thus has knowledge of Me as the Purushottama, - the Almighty - adores Me with Bhakti, with all-knowledge and in every way of his natural being.

Chapter 15, Verse 20

iti guhyatamaṁ śāstram
idam uktaṁ mayā'nagha
etad buddhvā buddhimān syāt
kṛta-kṛtyaś ca bhārata

Thus by Me the most secret shastra has been told, O sinless one. To know it absolutely is to be perfected in understanding and successful in the supreme sense, O Arjuna.

hariḥ oṁ tat sat
iti śrīmad bhagavad gītā sūpaniṣatsu
brahma vidyāyāṁ yoga śāstre śrī kṛṣṇārjuna
saṁvāde puruṣottama yogaḥ nāma
pañcadaśo 'dhyāyaḥ

Thus ends Chapter 15: Purushottama Yoga, from the dialogue between Sri Krishna and Arjuna in the *Upanishad* known as *Shreemad Bhagavad Gita*, the science of the Absolute, the yoga shastra.

CHAPTER 16
DAIVAASURASAMPAD VIBHAAGA YOGA

atha ṣoḍaśo 'dhyāyaḥ

Here begins the sixteenth chapter

Chapter 16, Verses 1-3

srī bhagavān uvāca
abhayaṁ sattva saṁśuddhiḥ
jñāna yoga vyavasthitaḥ
dānaṁ damaśca yajñāśca
svādhyāyas tapa ārjavam

ahiṁsā satyam akrodhas
tyāgaḥ śāntir apaiśunam
dayā bhūteṣv-aloluptaṁ
mārdavaṁ hrīr acāpalam

tejaḥ kṣamā dhṛtiḥ śaucam
adroho nātimānitā
bhavanti sampadaṁ daivīṁ
abhijātasya bhārata

The Lord says: Fearlessness, purity of mind, consistent contemplation on wisdom, philanthropy, self-control, worship, study of the *Vedas*, self-discipline, forthrightness, non-injury, truthfulness, freedom from anger, renunciation, tranquillity, freedom from slandering, compassion to all beings, freedom from hankering, gentleness, modesty, freedom from whimsicality; refulgence, forgiveness, fortitude, purity, freedom from spite and humility. These treasures, O Arjuna, belong to one who is born to the deva nature.

Chapter 16, Verse 4

dambho darpo'bhimānaśca
krodhaḥ pāruṣyam eva ca
ajñānaṁ cābhijātasya
pārtha sampadam āsurīm

Pride, arrogance, excessive self-esteem, wrath, harshness, ignorance, these, O Paartha, are the wealth of the man born into the asuric nature.

Chapter 16, Verse 5

daivī sampad vimokṣāya
nibandhāyāsurī matā
mā śucaḥ sampadaṁ daivīm
abhijāto'si pāṇḍava

The divine qualities lead towards liberation; the asuric towards bondage. Grieve not, for you are born in the deva nature, O Pandava.

Chapter 16, Verse 6

dvau bhūta sargau loke 'smin
daiva āsura eva ca
daivo vistaraśaḥ proktaḥ
āsuraṁ pārtha me śṛṇu

There are two creations of beings in this material world: the devic and the asuric. The devic has been described at length. Hear from Me, O Paartha, the asuric.

Chapter 16, Verse 7

pravṛttiṁ ca nivṛttiṁ ca
janā na vidurāsurāḥ
na śaucaṁ nāpi cācāro
na satyaṁ teṣu vidyate

Asuric men have no true knowledge of the way of action or the way of abstention; truth is not in them, nor clean doing, nor faithful observance.

Chapter 16, Verse 8

asatyam apratiṣṭhaṁ te
jagad-āhur anīśvaram
aparaspara sambhūtaṁ
kim anyat kāma haitukam

"The world is without God," they say, "not true, not founded in truth, brought about by mutual union, with desire for its sole cause, a world of chance."

Chapter 16, Verse 9

etāṁ dṛṣṭim avaṣṭabhya
naṣṭātmāno'lpa buddhayaḥ
prabhavanty-ugra karmāṇaḥ
kṣayāya jagato'hitāḥ

Leaning on that way of seeing life, and by its falsehood ruining their souls and their reason, the asuric people become the centre, or instrument, of a fierce, demonic, violent action, a power of destruction in the world, a fount of injury and evil.

Chapter 16, Verse 10

kāmam āśritya duṣpūraṁ
dambha māna madānvitāḥ
mohād gṛhītvāsadgrahān
pravartante 'śuci-vratāḥ

Resorting to insatiable desire, arrogant, full of self-esteem and the drunkenness of their pride, these misguided souls delude themselves, persist in false and obstinate aims and pursue the fixed impure resolution of their longings.

Chapter 16, Verse 11

cintām aparimeyāṁ ca
pralayāntām upāśritāḥ
kāmopabhoga paramā
etāvad iti niścitāḥ

They imagine that desire and enjoyment are all the aim of life and they are the prey of a devouring, measurelessly unceasing care and thought and endeavour and anxiety till the moment of their death.

Chapter 16, Verses 12-15

āśā-pāśa-śatair baddhāḥ
kāma krodha parāyaṇāḥ
īhante kāma bhogārtham
anyāyenārtha sañcayān

idam-adya mayā labdham
imaṁ prāpsye manoratham
idam astīdam api me
bhaviṣyati punar dhanam

asau mayā hataḥ śatrur
haniṣye cāparān api
īśvaro'ham ahaṁ bhogī
siddho'haṁ balavān sukhī

āṣyo'bhijanavān asmi
ko'nyosti sadṛśo mayā
yakṣye dāsyāmi modiṣye
ityajñāna vimohitāḥ

Bound by a hundred bonds, devoured by wrath and lust, untiringly occupied in amassing unjust gains which may serve their enjoyment and the satisfaction of their craving, always they think. "Today I have gained this object of desire, tomorrow I shall have that other; today I have so much wealth, more I will get tomorrow. I have killed this my enemy, the rest too I will kill. I am a lord and king of men, I am perfect, accomplished, strong, happy, fortunate, a privileged enjoyer of the world; I am wealthy, I am of high birth; who is there like unto me? I will sacrifice, I will give, I will enjoy."

Chapter 16, Verse 16

anekacitta vibhrāntā
moha-jāla-samāvṛtāḥ
prasaktāḥ kāma bhogeṣu
patanti narake'śucau

Thus occupied by many egoistic ideas, deluded, addicted to the gratification of desire doing works, but doing them wrongly, acting mightily, but for themselves, for desire, for enjoyment, not for God in themselves and God in man, they fall into the unclean hell of their own evil.

Chapter 16, Verse 17

ātma-saṁbhāvitāḥ stabdhā
dhana-māna-madānvitāḥ
yajante nāma yajñais te
dambhenāvidhi pūrvakam

They sacrifice and give not in the true order, but from a self-regarding ostentation, from vanity and with a stiff and foolish pride.

Chapter 16, Verse 18

ahaṅkāraṁ balaṁ darpaṁ
kāmaṁ krodhaṁ ca saṁśritāḥ
mām-ātma para-deheṣu
pradviṣanto'bhyasūyakāḥ

In the egoism of their strength and power, in the violence of their wrath and arrogance, they hate, despise and belittle the God hidden in themselves and the God in other people.

Chapter 16, Verse 19

tān ahaṁ dviṣataḥ krūrān
saṁsāreṣu narādhamān
kṣipāmy-ajasram aśubhān
āsurīṣveva yoniṣu

These proud haters, evil, cruel, vilest among men in the world, I cast down continually into more and more asuric births.

Chapter 16, Verse 20

āsurīṁ yonim āpannā
mūḍhā janmani janmani
mām aprāpyeva kaunteya
tato yānty-adhamāṁ gatim

Cast into asuric wombs, deluded birth after birth, they find Me not and sink down into the lowest status of soul nature.

Chapter 16, Verse 21

trividhaṁ narakasyedaṁ
dvāraṁ nāśanam ātmanaḥ
kāmaḥ krodhas tathā lobhas
tasmād etat trayaṁ tyajet

Threefold are the doors of Hell, destructive of the soul-desire, wrath and greed: therefore, let man renounce these three.

Chapter 16, Verse 22

etair vimuktaḥ kaunteya
tamo dvārais tribhir naraḥ
ācaraty ātmanaḥ śreyas
tato yāti parāṁ gatim

A man liberated from these doors of darkness, O son of Kunti, follows his own higher good and arrives at the highest soul-status.

Chapter 16, Verse 23

yaḥ śāstra vidhim utsṛjya
vartate kāma kārataḥ
na sa siddhim avāpnoti
na sukhaṁ na parāṁ gatim

He who, having cast aside the rules of the shastras, follows the promptings of desire, attains not to perfection, nor happiness, nor the highest soul-status.

Chapter 16, Verse 24

tasmāt śāstra pramāṇaṁ te
kāryākārya vyavasthitau
jñātvā śāstra vidhān-oktaṁ
karma kartum ihārhasi

Therefore, let the shastras be your authority in determining what ought to be done or what ought not to be done. Knowing what has been declared by the rules of the shastras, you ought to work in this world.

hariḥ oṁ tat sat
iti śrīmad bhagavad gītā sūpaniṣatsu
brahma vidyāyāṁ yoga śāstre śrī kṛṣṇārjuna
saṁvāde daivāsurasampad vibhāga yogaḥ
nāma ṣoḍaśo 'dhyāyaḥ

Thus ends Chapter 16: Daivaasurasampad Vibhaaga Yoga, from the dialogue between Sri Krishna and Arjuna in the *Upanishad* known as *Shreemad Bhagavad Gita*, the science of the Absolute, the yoga shastra.

CHAPTER 17
SHRADDHAATRAYA VIBHAAGA YOGA

atha saptadaśo 'dhyāyaḥ

Here begins the seventeenth chapter

Chapter 17, Verse1

arjuna uvāca
ye śāstra vidhim utsṛjya
yajante śraddhayānvitāḥ
teṣāṁ niṣṭhā tu kā kṛṣṇa
satvam āho rajas tamaḥ

Arjuna says: When people sacrifice to God or the demigods with faith, but abandon the rule of the shastras, what is that concentrated will of devotion in them, known as nishtha, which gives them this faith and moves them to this kind of action, O Krishna? Is it sattva, rajas or tamas?

Chapter 17, Verse 2

śrī bhagavān uvāca
trividhā bhavati śraddhā
dehināṁ sā svabhāvajā
sāttvikī rājasī caiva
tāmasī ceti tāṁ śṛṇu

The Lord says: The faith in embodied beings is of a triple kind like all things in Nature and varies according to the dominating quality of their nature, sattva, rajas or tamas. Hear you of these.

Chapter 17, Verse 3

sattvānurūpā sarvasya
śraddhā bhavati bhārata
śraddhāmayo'yaṁ puruṣo
yo yacchraddhaḥ sa eva saḥ

The faith of each one takes the shape given to it by one's character, O Arjuna. This Purusha, this soul in one, is, as it were, made of shraddha, a faith, a will to be a belief in itself and existence, and whatever is that faith, one is that and that is one.

Chapter 17, Verse 4

yajante sāttvikā devān
yakṣa rakṣāṁsi rājasāḥ
pretān bhūtagaṇāṁścānye
yajante tāmasā janāḥ

Sattvic people offer sacrifice to the deities, the rajasic to the yakshas (the keepers of wealth) and the rakshasic forces, the others, the tamasic, offer their sacrifice to elemental powers and grosser spirits.

Chapter 17, Verse 5-6

aśāstra vihitaṁ ghoraṁ
tapyante ye tapo janāḥ
dambhāhaṅkāra saṁyuktāḥ
kāma rāga balānvitāḥ

karṣayantaḥ śarīrasthaṁ
bhūta-grāmam acetasaḥ
māṁ caivāntaḥ śarīrasthaṁ
tān viddhyāsura niścayān

Those who perform violent austerities, contrary to the shastras, with arrogance and egoism, impelled by the force of their desires and passions, those of unripe minds tormenting the aggregated elements forming the body and troubling Me also, seated in the body, know these to be asuric in their resolves.

Chapter 17, Verse 7

āhāras-tvapi sarvasya
trividho bhavati priyaḥ
yajñas tapas tathā dānaṁ
teṣāṁ bhedam imaṁ śṛṇu

The food also which is dear to each is of triple character, as also sacrifice, asceticism and giving. Hear you the distinction of these.

Chapter 17, Verse 8

āyuḥ sattva bal-ārogya
sukha prīti vivardhanāḥ
rasyāḥ snigdhāḥ sthirā hṛdyā
āhārāḥ sāttvika priyāḥ

The sattvic temperament in the mental and physical body turns naturally to the things that increase the life, increase the inner and outer strength, nourish at once the mental, vital and physical force and increase the pleasure and satisfaction and happy condition of mind and life and body, all that is succulent and soft and firm and satisfying.

Chapter 17, Verse 9

kaṭvamla lavaṇāty-uṣṇa
tīkṣṇa rūkṣa vidāhinaḥ
āhārāḥ rājasasyeṣṭā
duḥkha śokāmaya pradāḥ

The rajasic temperament prefers naturally food that is violently sour, pungent, hot, acrid, rough and strong and burning, the aliments that increase ill-health and the distempers of the mind and body.

Chapter 17, Verse 10

yāta-yāmaṁ gata-rasaṁ
pūti paryuṣitaṁ ca yat
ucchiṣṭam api cāmedhyaṁ
bhojanaṁ tāmasa priyam

The tamasic temperament takes a perverse pleasure in cold, impure, stale, rotten or tasteless food or even, like the animals, accepts the remnants half-eaten by others.

Chapter 17, Verse 11

aphalā-kāṅkṣibhir yajño
vidhi dṛṣṭo ya ijyate
yaṣṭavyam eveti manaḥ
samādhāma sa sāttvikaḥ

The sacrifice which is offered by people without desire for personal rewards, which is executed according to the right principle of the shastras, and with concentrated mind, that is sattvic.

Chapter 17, Verse12

abhisandhāya tu phalaṁ
dambhārtham api caiva yat
ijyate bharata-śreṣṭha
taṁ yajñaṁ viddhi rājasam

The sacrifice offered with a view to the personal rewards, and also for ostentation, O Arjuna, know that to be of a rajasic nature.

Chapter 17, Verse 13

vidhi hīnam asṛṣṭānnaṁ
mantra-hīnam adakṣiṇam
śraddhā virahitaṁ yajñaṁ
tāmasaṁ paricakṣate

The sacrifice not performed according to the right rule of the shastras, without giving of food, without the mantra, without gifts, empty of faith, is said to be tamasic.

Chapter 17, Verse 14

deva dvija guru prājña
pūjanaṁ śaucam ārjavam
brahmacaryam ahiṁsā ca
śārīraṁ tapa ucyate

Adoration of the deities, the twice-born, the preceptors, the enlightened ones, purity, rectitude, chastity and non-injury, these are said to be the physical disciplines.

Chapter 17, Verse 15

anudvega-karaṁ vākyaṁ
satyaṁ priya-hitaṁ ca yat
svādhyāyābhyasanaṁ caiva
vāṅmayaṁ tapa ucyate

Speech causing no trouble to others, true, kind and beneficial, the study of scripture, are called the disciplines of speech.

Chapter 17, Verse 16

manaḥ prasādaḥ saumyatvaṁ
maunam ātma vinigrahaḥ
bhāva saṁśuddhir ityetat
tapo mānasam ucyate

A clear and calm gladness of mind, gentleness, silence, self-control, the purifying of the whole temperament - this is called the discipline of the mind.

Chapter 17, Verse 17

śraddhayā parayā taptaṁ
tapas tat trividhaṁ naraiḥ
aphalākāṅkṣibhir yuktaiḥ
sāttvikaṁ paricakṣate

This threefold discipline, done with a highest enlightened faith, with no desire for fruit, harmonised, is said to be sattvic.

Chapter 17, Verse 18

satkāra māna pūjārthaṁ
tapo dambhena caiva yat
kriyate tad iha proktaṁ
rājasaṁ calam adhruvam

The discipline which is undertaken to get honour and worship from people, for the sake of outward glory and greatness and for ostentation is said to be rajasic, unstable and fleeting.

Chapter 17, Verse 19

mūḍha-grāheṇātmano yat
pīḍayā kriyate tapaḥ
parasyotsādanārthaṁ vā
tat tāmasam udāhṛtam

That discipline which is pursued under a clouded and deluded idea, performed with effort and suffering imposed on oneself of else with concentration of the energy in a will to hurt others, that is said to be tamasic.

Chapter 17, Verse 20

dātavyam iti yad-dānaṁ
dīyate 'nupakāriṇe
deśe kāle ca pātre ca
tad-dānaṁ sāttvikaṁ smṛtam

The charity that is dispensed from a sense of duty, to one who does not reciprocate, at the proper place and time to a deserving person - that is said to be sattvic.

Chapter 17, Verse 21

yattu pratyupakārārthaṁ
phalam uddiśya vā punaḥ
dīyate ca parikliṣṭaṁ
tad-dānaṁ rājasaṁ smṛtam

But that which is given as a consideration for something received or in expectation of future reward, or grudgingly (something which is given with an expectation), is considered to be rajasic.

Chapter 17, Verse 22

adeśakāle yad-dānam
apātrebhyaśca dīyate
asat-kṛtam avajñātaṁ
tat-tāmasam udāhṛtam

That gift which is given at the wrong place and at the wrong time to unworthy recipients, without due respect and with derision, is considered to be tamasic.

Chapter 17, Verse 23

oṁ tat sad iti nirdeśo
brahmaṇas trividhaḥ smṛtaḥ
brāhmaṇas tena vedāś ca
yajñāś ca vihitāḥ purā

The formula *Om Tat Sat* is the triple definition of the Brahman, by whom the Brahmins, the *Vedas* and sacrifices were created of old.

Chapter 17, Verse 24

tasmād om-ity-udāhṛtya
yajña dāna tapaḥ kriyāḥ
pravartante vidhān-oktāḥ
satataṁ brahma-vādinām

Therefore, with the pronunciation of *'Om'* the acts of sacrifice, giving and self-discipline, as laid down in the rules, are always commenced by the knowers of the Brahman.

Chapter 17, Verse 25

tad-ity-anabhisandhāya
phalaṁ yajña-tapaḥ kriyāḥ
dāna kriyāśca vividhāḥ
kriyante mokṣa-kāṅkṣibhiḥ

With the pronunciation of *Tat* and without desire of fruit are performed the various acts of sacrifice, self-discipline and giving by the seekers of liberation.

Chapter 17, Verse 26

sad-bhāve sādhu-bhāve ca
sad-ity-etat prayujyate
praśaste karmaṇi tathā
sacchabdaḥ pārtha yujyate

Sat means good, and it means existence; likewise, O Paartha, the word *Sat* is used in the sense of a good work.

Chapter 17, Verse 27

yajñe tapasi dāne ca
sthitiḥ sad-iti cocyate
karma caiva tadarthīyaṁ
sad-ityevābhidhīyate

Perseverance in sacrifice, self-discipline and charity is also called *Sat*, and so also any action for the sake of these is termed *Sat*.

Chapter 17, Verse 28

aśraddhayā hutaṁ dattaṁ
tapas taptaṁ kṛtaṁ ca yat
asad ity-ucyate pārtha
na ca tat pretya no iha

Whatever is wrought (done) without faith, oblation, giving, self-discipline or other work, is called *Asat*, O Paartha; it is worthless, here or hereafter.

hariḥ oṁ tat sat
iti śrīmad bhagavad gītā sūpaniṣatsu
brahma vidyāyāṁ yoga śāstre śrī kṛṣṇārjuna
saṁvāde śraddhātraya vibhāga yogaḥ nāma
saptadaśo 'dhyāyaḥ

Thus ends Chapter 17: Shraddhaatraya Vibhaaga Yoga, from the dialogue between Sri Krishna and Arjuna in the *Upanishad* known as *Shreemad Bhagavad Gita*, the science of the Absolute, the yoga shastra.

CHAPTER 18
MOKSHA SANNYASA YOGA

athāṣṭādaśo 'dhyāyaḥ

Here begins the eighteenth chapter

Chapter 18, Verse 1

arjuna uvāca
saṁnyāsasya mahābāho
tattvam icchāmi veditum
tyāgasya ca hṛṣīkeśa
pṛthak keśiniṣūdanam

Arjuna says: I desire to know the decisive truth about the difference between renunciation (Sannyas) and relinquishment (tyaga) O Krishna.

Chapter 18, Verse 2

śrī bhagavān uvāca
kāmyānāṁ karmaṇāṁ nyāsaṁ
sannyāsaṁ kavayo viduḥ
sarva karma phala tyāgaṁ
prāhus tyāgaṁ vicakṣaṇāḥ

The Lord says: The enlightened ones understand that renunciation (Sannyas) means the giving up of all works which are motivated by desire. The wise declare relinquishment (tyaga) to be the relinquishment of the fruits of all works.

Chapter 18, Verse 3

tyājyaṁ doṣavad ityeke
karma prāhur manīṣiṇaḥ
yajñā dāna tapaḥ karma
na tyājyam iti cāpare

Some learned ones say that all actions should be given up as defective; others declare that works such as yagna, philanthropy and self-discipline should not be given up.

Chapter 18, Verse 4

niścayaṁ śrṇu me tatra
tyāge bharata sattama
tyāgo hi puruṣa-vyāghra
tri-vidhaḥ saṁprakīrtitaḥ

Listen to My verdict, O Arjuna, regarding relinquishment (tyaga) for relinquishment is declared to be of three kinds.

Chapter 18, Verse 5

yajña dāna tapaḥ karma
na tyājyaṁ kāryam eva tat
yajño dānaṁ tapaścaiva
pāvanāni manīṣiṇām

Acts of sacrifice, giving and self-discipline ought not to be renounced at all, but should be performed, for they purify the wise.

Chapter 18, Verse 6

etānyapi tu karmāṇi
saṅgaṁ tvyaktvā phalāni ca
kartavyānīti me pārthas
niścitaṁ matam uttamam

Even these actions certainly ought to be done, O Paartha, leaving aside attachment and fruit.

Chapter 18, Verse 7

niyatasya tu saṁnyāsaḥ
karmaṇo nopapadyate
mohāt tasya parityāgas
tāmasaḥ parikīrtitaḥ

Verily, renunciation of rightly regulated actions is not proper, to renounce them from ignorance is a tamasic renunciation.

Chapter 18, Verse 8

duḥkham ityeva yat karma
kāya kleśa-bhayāt tyajet
sa kṛtvā rājasaṁ tyāgaṁ
naiva tyāga phalaṁ labhet

The one who gives up works because they bring sorrow or are a trouble to the flesh, thus doing rajasic renunciation, obtain not the fruit of renunciation.

Chapter 18, Verse 9

kāryam ityeva yat karma
niyataṁ kriyate'rjuna
saṅgaṁ tyaktvā phalaṁ caiva
sa tyāgaḥ sāttviko mataḥ

The one who performs a rightly regulated action (allocated duty), because it has to be done, without any attachment either to the action or to the fruit of the action, that renunciation is regarded as sattvic.

Chapter 18, Verse 10

na dveṣṭy-akuśalaṁ karma
kuśale nānuṣajjate
tyāgī sattva samāviṣṭo
medhāvī chinna-saṁśayaḥ

The wise one with doubts cast away, who renounces in the light of the full sattvic mind, has no aversion to unpleasant action, nor attachment to pleasant action.

Chapter 18, Verse 11

na hi deha-bhṛtā śakyaṁ
tyaktuṁ karmāṇy-aśeṣataḥ
yastu karma-phala-tyāgī
sa tyāgīty-abhidhīyate

Nor indeed can embodied beings renounce all works; verily the one, who gives up the fruit of action, is said to be a tyagi.

Chapter 18, Verse 12

anistam istaṁ miśraṁ ca
trividhaṁ karmaṇaḥ phalam
bhavaty-atyāgināṁ pretya
na tu saṁnyāsināṁ kvacit

The three kinds of result, pleasant, unpleasant and mixed, in this or other worlds, in this or another life are for the slaves of desire and ego; these things do not cling to the free spirit.

Chapter 18, Verse 13

pañcaitāni mahābāho
kāraṇāni nibodha me
sāṅkhye kṛtānte proktāni
siddhaye sarva karmaṇām

These five causes, O Arjuna, learn of Me as laid down by the Sankhya for the accomplishment of all works.

Chapter 18, Verse 14

adhiṣṭhānaṁ tathā kartā
karaṇaṁ ca pṛthag vidham
vividhāśca pṛthak-ceṣṭā
daivaṁ caivātra pañcamam

The seat of action (the body) and likewise the agent, the various organs, the different and distinctive kinds of endeavours and finally destiny is the fifth among these.

Chapter 18, Verse 15

śarīra vāṅg-manobhir yat
karma prārabhate naraḥ
nyāyyaṁ vā viparītaṁ vā
pañcaite tasya hetavaḥ

For whatever work one undertakes by body, speech and mind, whether right or wrong, these five are its basis.

Chapter 18, Verse 16

tatraivaṁ sati kartāram
ātmānaṁ kevalaṁ tu yaḥ
paśyat yat kṛta buddhitvān
na sa paśyati durmatiḥ

Now such being the case, the one who sees oneself as the only doer is a fool on account of undeveloped intellect – does not see at all.

Chapter 18, Verse 17

yasya nāhaṅkṛto bhāvo
buddhir yasya na lipyate
hatvāpi sa imāṁ llokān
na hanti na nibadhyate

The one who is free from the ego-sense, whose intelligence is not affected, though one slays these people, one slays not, nor is bound by one's actions.

Chapter 18, Verse 18

jñānaṁ jñeyaṁ pari-jñātā
trividhā karma codanā
karaṇaṁ karma karteti
trividhaḥ karma saṅgrahaḥ

Knowledge, the object of knowledge and the knower, these three things constitute the mental impulsion to work; there are again three things, the doer, the instrument and the work done, that hold the action together and make it possible.

Chapter 18, Verse 19

jñānaṁ karma cha kartā cha
tridhaiva gunabhedatah
prochyate gunasankhyāne
yathāvachchhirnu tānyapi

Knowledge, work and doer are of three kinds, says the sankhya (renunciate), according to the difference in the gunas (qualities); hear duly these also.

Chapter 18, Verse 20

sarva-bhūteṣu yenaikaṁ
bhāvam avyayam īkṣate
avibhaktaṁ vibhakteṣu
taj-jñānaṁ viddhi sāttvikam

That knowledge which reveals one immutable reality in all beings, and not as separate in the different bodies - know that knowledge to be sattvic.

Chapter 18, Verse 21

pṛthaktvena tu yaj-jñānaṁ
nānā bhāvān pṛthag-vidhān
vetti sarveṣu bhūteṣu
taj-jñānaṁ viddhi rājasam

But that knowledge which sees various and distinctive (spiritual) entities in all the separate (physical) beings - know that knowledge to be rajasic.

Chapter 18, Verse 22

yat tu kṛtsnavad ekasmin
kārye saktam ahaitukam
atattvārthavad alpaṁ ca
tat tāmasam udāhṛtam

But that which adheres to one single act as if it were the whole, which is not founded on reason, and which is untrue and trivial - that knowledge is declared to be tamasic.

Chapter 18, Verse 23

niyataṁ saṅga rahitam
arāga-dveṣataḥ kṛtam
aphala prepsunā karma
yat tat sāttvikam ucyate

All action which is dutiful, performed without attachment, without liking or disliking, done by one not desirous of fruit, that is called sattvic.

Chapter 18, Verse 24

yat tu kāmepsunā karma
sāhaṅkāreṇa vā punaḥ
kriyate bahulāyāsaṁ
tad rājasam-udāhṛtam

But that action which one undertakes under the dominion of desire, or with an egoistic sense of one's own personality in the action, and which is done with inordinate effort, that is declared to be rajasic.

Chapter 18, Verse 25

anubandhaṁ kṣayaṁ hinsām
anavekṣya ca pauruṣam
mohād ārabhyate karma
yat tat tāmasam ucyate

That task which is undertaken through delusion, disregarding the consequences, loss, injury and one's own capacity is said to be tamasic.

Chapter 18, Verse 26

mukta saṅgo'nahaṁvādī
dhṛty-utsāha-samanvitaḥ
siddhy-asiddhyor nirvikāraḥ
kartā sāttvika ucyate

An agent who is free from attachment, and self-acclaim, who is endowed with perseverance and enthusiasm and is unaffected by success and failure, is said to be sattvic.

Chapter 18, Verse 27

rāgī karma phala prepsuḥ
lubdho hiṁsātmako'śuciḥ
harṣa śokānvitaḥ kartā
rājasaḥ parikīrtitaḥ

Eagerly attached to the work, passionately desirous of fruit, greedy, impure, often violent and cruel and brutal in the means one uses, full of joy (in success) and grief (in failure) such an agent is known as rajasic.

Chapter 18, Verse 28

ayuktaḥ prākṛtaḥ stabdhaḥ
śaṭho naiṣkṛtiko'lasaḥ
viṣādī dīrgha-sūtrī ca
kartā tāmasa ucyate

One who acts with a mechanical mind, is stupid, obstinate, cunning, insolent, lazy, easily depressed, procrastinating (delaying, indecisive), that doer is called tamasic.

Chapter 18, Verse 29

buddher bhedaṁ dhṛteścaiva
guṇatas trividhaṁ śṛṇu
procyamānam aśeṣeṇa
pṛthaktvena dhanañjaya

Hear now, the threefold division of buddhi (rationalism) and dhriti (fortitude), according to the gunas, O Arjuna, as I declare them completely and distinctly.

Chapter 18, Verse 30

pravṛtiṁ ca nivṛttiṁ ca
kāryākārye bhayābhaye
bandhaṁ mokṣaṁ ca yā vetti
buddhiḥ sā pārtha sāttvikī

That rationalism is considered to be sattvic O Arjuna, which discerns extroversion and introversion, what ought to be done and what ought not to be done, fear and freedom from fear, bondage and liberation.

Chapter 18, Verse 31

yayā dharmam adharmaṁ ca
kāryaṁ cākāryam eva ca
ayathāvat prajānāti
buddhiḥ sā pārtha rājasī

The rationalism which produces a mistaken conception of dharma and adharma and also of what ought to be done and what ought not to be done, O Arjuna, is rajasic.

Chapter 18, Verse 32

adharmaṁ dharmam iti yā
manyate tamasāvṛtā
sarvārthān viparītāṁśca
buddhiḥ sā pārtha tāmasī

That rationalism, O Arjuna, which, enveloped in darkness, regards adharma as dharma and which reverses every value, is tamasic.

Chapter 18, Verse 33

dhṛtyā yayā dhārayate
manaḥ prāṇendriya kriyāḥ
yogenāvyabhicāriṇyā
dhṛtiḥ sā pārtha sāttvikī

That unwavering persistence by which, through yoga, one controls the mind, the senses and the life, that persistence, O Paartha, is sattvic.

Chapter 18, Verse 34

yayā tu dharma kāmārthān
dhṛtyā dhārayate'rjuna
prasaṅgena phalākāṅkṣī
dhṛtiḥ sā pārtha rājasī

That perseverance, O Arjuna, by which, on account of attachment and desire for rewards, one adheres to the pursuit of dharma, kama and artha is rajasic.

Chapter 18, Verse 35

yayā svapnaṁ bhayaṁ śokaṁ
viṣādaṁ madam eva ca
na vimuñcati durmedhā
dhṛtiḥ sā pārtha tāmasī

That perseverance by which a foolish person does not give up sleep, fear, grief, depression and passion, O Arjuna, is of the nature of tamas.

Chapter 18, Verses 36-37

sukhaṁ tvidānīṁ trividhaṁ
śṛṇu me bharatarṣabha
abhyāsād ramate yatra
duḥkhāntaṁ ca nigacchati

yat tad agre viṣam iva
pariṇāme 'mṛtopamam
tat sukhaṁ sāttvikaṁ proktam
ātma buddhi prasādajam

Now hear from Me, O Arjuna, the threefold division of happiness, in which one enjoys by continued practice and by which one is surely freed from suffering; that joy which is like poison at first but eventually becomes like ambrosia - the Churning of the Milky Ocean -, arising from the serene state of the mind focusing on the Atma - such joy is said to be sattvic.

Chapter 18, Verse 38

viṣayendriya saṁyogād
yat tad agre'mṛtopamam
pariṇāme viṣam iva
tat sukhaṁ rājasaṁ smṛtam

That pleasure which arises from contact of the sense organs with their objects, which at first is like ambrosia but in the end like poison - that is declared to be rajasic.

Chapter 18, Verse 39

yad agre cānubandhe ca
sukhaṁ mohanam ātmanaḥ
nidrālasya pramādotthaṁ
tat tāmasam udāhṛtam

That pleasure which is characterised by self-delusion both in the beginning and the sequel, arising from sleep, indolence and negligence is declared to be tamasic.

Chapter 18, Verse 40

na tad asti pṛthivyāṁ vā
divi deveṣu vā punaḥ
sattvaṁ prakṛti-jair muktaṁ
yad ebhiḥ syāt tribhir guṇaiḥ

There is not an entity, either on the Earth or again in Heaven among the gods, that is not subject to the workings of these three qualities (gunas), born of Nature.

Chapter 18, Verse 41

brāhmaṇa kṣatriya viśāṁ
śūdrāṇāṁ ca parantapa
karmāṇi pravibhaktāni
svabhāva prabhavair guṇaiḥ

The duties of the brahmins, kshatriyas, vaishyas and shudras, O Arjuna, are distinctly divided according to their inherent dispositions.

Chapter 18, Verse 42

śamo damas tapaḥ śaucaṁ
kṣāntir ārjavam eva ca
jñānaṁ vijñānam āstikyaṁ
brahmam-karma svabhāvajam

Serenity and restraint, self-discipline, purity, forbearance, integrity, wisdom, insight and faith in the *Vedas* - all these constitute the functions of the brahmins based on their inherent disposition.

Chapter 18, Verse 43

śauryaṁ tejo dhṛtir dākṣyaṁ
yuddhe cāpyapalāyanam
dānam īśvara-bhāvaśca
kṣātraṁ karma svabhāvajam

Valour, power, determination, proficiency and courage in battle, generosity and leadership are the inherent characteristics of a kshatriya.

Chapter 18, Verse 44

kṛṣi gau-rakṣya vāṇijyaṁ
vaiśya-karma svabhāvajam
paricaryātmakaṁ karma
śūdrasyāpi svabhāvajam

Agriculture, cattle-breeding and trade are the innate vocations of the vaishyas, and the duty of the shudras is service, arising from their innate dispositions.

Chapter 18, Verse 45

sve sve karmaṇy-abhirataḥ
saṁsiddhiṁ labhate naraḥ
svakarma nirataḥ siddhiṁ
yathā vindati tacchṛṇu

Those who are engaged in their own natural work attain perfection. Listen how perfection is won by those who are content in their own natural work.

Chapter 18, Verse 46

yataḥ pravṛttir bhūtānāṁ
yena sarvam idaṁ tatam
svakarmaṇā tam abhyarcya
siddhiṁ vindati mānavaḥ

He from whom all beings originate, by whom all this universe is pervaded, by worshipping Him by their own work, people reach perfection.

Chapter 18, Verse 47

śreyān svadharmo viguṇaḥ
para-dharmāt svanuṣṭhitāt
svabhāva niyataṁ karma
kurvan-nāpnoti kilbiṣam

Better is one's own dharma, even when imperfectly done, than the dharma of another well-performed. When one practices the dharma ordained by one's own nature, one incurs no fault.

Chapter 18, Verse 48

sahajaṁ karma kaunteya
sadoṣam api na tyajet
sarvārambhā hi doṣeṇa
dhūmenāgnir ivāvṛtāḥ

One should not relinquish one's natural vocational skills, O Arjuna, though they may be imperfect, for all undertakings are enveloped by imperfection like fire by smoke.

Chapter 18, Verse 49

asakta buddhiḥ sarvatra
jitātmā vigata spṛhaḥ
naiṣkarmya siddhiṁ paramāṁ
sannyāsenādhigacchati

One who is completely unattached, who is self-controlled and is free from desires, attains by renunciation the supreme perfection of liberation from all activity.

Chapter 18, Verse 50

siddhiṁ prāpto yathā brahma
tathāpnoti nibodha me
samāsenaiva kaunteya
niṣṭhā jñānasya yā parā

Learn from Me in brief, O Arjuna, how one who has achieved perfection, attains Brahman, Self-Realisation, which is the supreme consummation of wisdom.

Chapter 18, Verses 51-53

buddhyā viśuddhayā yukto
dhṛtyātmānaṁ niyamya ca
śabdādīn viṣayāṁs-tyaktvā
rāga-dveṣau vyudasya ca

vivikta-sevī laghvāśī
yata-vāk-kāya-mānasaḥ
dhyāna yoga paro nityaṁ
vairāgyaṁ samupāśritaḥ

ahaṅkāraṁ balaṁ darpaṁ
kāmaṁ krodhaṁ parigraham
vimucya nirmamaḥ śānto
brahma-bhūyāya kalpate

Uniting the purified intelligence with the pure spiritual substance in us, controlling the whole being by firm and steady will (sadhana), having renounced sound and the other objects of the senses - entering the deep calmness - withdrawing from all liking and disliking, resorting to impersonal solitude, moderate speech, body and mind controlled, constantly united with the inmost Self by meditation, completely giving up desire and attachment, having put away egoism, violence, arrogance, desire, wrath, the sense and instinct of possession, free from all notions of 'I' and 'my', calm and luminously impassive - one is fit to become the Brahman.

Chapter 18, Verse 54

brahma-bhūtaḥ prasannātmā
na śocati na kāṅkṣati
samaḥ sarveṣu bhūteṣu
mad-bhaktiṁ labhate parām

When one has become the Brahman; when one, serene in the Self, neither grieves nor desires; when one is equal to all beings, then one gets the supreme Love and devotion to Me.

Chapter 18, Verse 55

bhaktyā mām abhijānāti
yāvān yaścāsmi tattvataḥ
tato māṁ tattvato jñātvā
viśate tad anantaram

By Bhakti he comes to know Me, who and how much I am and in all the reality and principles of My Being; having thus known Me, he enters into That (Purushottama).

Chapter 18, Verse 56

sarva karmāṇyapi sadā
kurvāṇo mad vyapāśrayaḥ
mat prasādād avāpnoti
śāśvataṁ padam avyayam

And by doing also all actions always lodged in Me, he attains by My Grace the eternal and imperishable status.

Chapter 18, Verse 57

cetasā sarva karmāṇi
mayi saṁnyasya mat paraḥ
buddhi-yogam upāśritya
mac-cittaḥ satataṁ bhava

Devoting all yourself to Me, giving up in your conscious mind all your actions into Me, resorting to the Yoga of Discrimination (Buddhi Yoga), be always one in heart and consciousness with Me.

Chapter 18, Verse 58

mac-cittaḥ sarva durgāṇi
mat-prasādāt tariṣyasi
atha cettvam ahaṅkārān
na śrosyasi vinaṅkṣyasi

If you are one in heart and consciousness with Me at all times, then by My Grace you shall pass safe through all difficult and perilous passages; but if from egoism you hear not, you shall fall into perdition.

Chapter 18, Verse 59

yad ahaṅkāram āśritya
na yotsya iti manyase
mithyaiṣa vyavasāyaste
prakṛtis-tvāṁ niyokṣyati

If out of self-conceit, you think; 'I will not fight,' your resolve is futile – Prakriti will compel you.

Chapter 18, Verse 60

svabhāvajane kaunteya
nibaddhaḥ svena karmaṇā
kartuṁ necchasi yan mohāt
kariṣyasy-avaśo'pi tat

O Arjuna, bound by your own karma inborn in your own nature, having no self-control, you will be compelled to do that very thing which, through delusion, you now desire not to do.

Chapter 18, Verse 61

īśvaraḥ sarva bhūtānāṁ
hṛddeśe'rjuna tiṣṭhati
bhrāmayan sarva-bhūtāni
yantrārūḍhāni māyayā

The Lord, O Arjuna, is seated in the heart of all beings, turning all beings as if mounted upon a machine by His Maya.

Chapter 18, Verse 62

tam-eva śaraṇaṁ gaccha
sarva-bhāvena bhārata
tat prasādāt parāṁ śāntiṁ
sthānaṁ prāpsyasi śāśvatam

In Him take refuge in every way of your being and by His Grace you shall come to the supreme peace and the eternal status.

Chapter 18, Verse 63

iti te jñānam ākhyātaṁ
guhyād guhyataraṁ mayā
vimṛśyaitad aśeṣeṇa
yathecchasi tathā kuru

So have I expounded to you a knowledge more secret than that which is hidden; having reflected on it fully, do as you would.

Chapter 18, Verse 64

sarva guhyatamaṁ bhūyaḥ
śṛṇu me paramaṁ vacaḥ
iṣṭo'si me dṛṣam iti
tato vakṣyāmi te hitam

Further hear the most secret, the supreme word that I shall speak to you; beloved you are intimately of Me, therefore will I speak for your good.

Chapter 18, Verse 65

manmanā bhava mad-bhakto
mad yājī māṁ namas kuru
mām evaiṣyasi satyaṁ te
pratijāne priyo'si me

Focus your mind on Me, be devoted to Me, worship Me, prostrate before Me and you shall come to Me alone. I promise you this verily, for you are dear to Me.

Chapter 18, Verse 66

sarva dharmān parityajya
mām ekaṁ śaraṇaṁ vraja
ahaṁ tvā sarva-pāpebhyo
mokṣayiṣyāmi mā śucaḥ

Abandon all dharmas and take refuge in Me alone. I will deliver you from all sin and evil, do not grieve.

Chapter 18, Verse 67

idaṁ te nātapaskāya
nābhaktāya kadācana
na cāśuśrūṣave vācyaṁ
na ca māṁ yo'bhyasūyasi

Never is this to be spoken by you to one without self-discipline, not to one that is not devoted and not to him who does no service; nor yet to him who despises and belittles Me when I am lodged in the human body.

Chapter 18, Verse 68

ya imaṁ paraṁ guhyaṁ
mad bhakteṣv-abhidhāsyati
bhaktiṁ mayi parāṁ kṛtvā
mām evaiṣyaty-asaṁśayaḥ

One, who possessed of supreme devotion to Me, expounds this highest mystery to My devotees, shall come to Me, there is no doubt about this.

Chapter 18, Verse 69

na ca tasmān manuṣyeṣu
kaścin me priya-kṛttamaḥ
bhavitā na ca me tasmād
anyaḥ priyataro bhuvi

Nor is there among human beings anyone who does more precious service to Me. Nor shall there be another on Earth dearer to Me than he.

Chapter 18, Verse 70

adhyeṣyete ca ya imaṁ
dharmyaṁ saṁvādam āvayoḥ
jñāna-yajñena tenāham
iṣṭaḥ syām iti me matiḥ

And whoever studies this dialogue of ours about dharma, worships Me through the sacrifice of knowledge (Jyaana yagna); such is My conviction.

Chapter 18, Verse 71

śraddhāvān anasūyaśca
śṛṇuyād api yo naraḥ
so'pi muktaḥ śubhāṁ lokān
prāpnuyāt puṇya karmaṇām

And the one who listens to it with faith and free from envy, shall also be liberated and will attain the auspicious realms of those who have performed meritorious deeds.

Chapter 18, Verse 72

kaccid etacchātaṁ pārtha
tvayaikāgreṇa cetasā
kaccid ajñāna saṁmohaḥ
pranaṣṭaste dhanañjaya

Have you paid attention to this, O Arjuna, with a concentrated mind? Has your delusion, caused by ignorance been dispelled?

Chapter 18, Verse 73

arjuna uvāca
naṣṭo mohaḥ smṛtir labdhā
tvat prasādān mayācyuta
sthito'smi gata sandehaḥ
kariṣye vacanaṁ tava

Arjuna says: Destroyed is my delusion, I have regained memory and insight (smriti) through Your Grace, O Infallible One. I am firm, dispelled are my doubts. I will act according to Your word.

Chapter 18, Verse 74

sañjaya uvāca
ity-ahaṁ vāsudevasya
pārthasya ca mahātmanaḥ
saṁvādam imam aśrauṣam
adbhutaṁ roma-harṣaṇam

Sanjaya says (to the blind king, Dhritarashtra): Thus have I heard this astounding dialogue between Vasudeva and the great-minded Arjuna, which makes my hair stand on end.

Chapter 18, Verse 75

vyāsa prasādāc-chātvān
etad guhyam aham param
yogaṁ yogeśvarāt kṛṣṇāt
sākṣāt kathayataḥ svayam

Through the Grace of Vyasa I heard this supreme secret, this yoga directly from Krishna, the Lord of yoga, who Himself declared it.

Chapter 18, Verse 76

rājan saṁsmṛtya saṁsmṛtya
saṁvādam imam adbhutam
keśavārjunayoḥ puṇyaṁ
hṛṣyāmi ca muhurmuhuḥ

O king, remembering this wonderful and sacred discourse of Keshava and Arjuna, I rejoice again and again.

Chapter 18, Verse 77

tacca saṁsmṛtya saṁsmṛtya
rūpam aty-adbhutaṁ hareḥ
vismayo me mahān rājan
hṛṣyāmi ca punaḥ punaḥ

Remembering also that most marvellous form of Hari, great is my wonder. O king, I rejoice, again and again.

Chapter 18, Verse 78

yatra yogeśvaraḥ kṛṣṇo
yatra pārtho dhanurdharaḥ
tatra śrīrvijayo bhūtir
dhruvā nītir matir mama

Wherever is Krishna, the Lord of yoga, wherever is Paartha, the archer, assured are there glory, victory and prosperity, and there also is the immutable Law of Right.

hariḥ oṁ tat sat
iti śrīmad bhagavad gītā sūpaniṣatsu
brahma vidyāyāṁ yoga śāstre śrī kṛṣṇārjuna
saṁvāde mokṣa saṁnyāsa yogaḥ nāma
athāṣṭādaśo 'dhyāyaḥ

Thus ends Chapter 18: Moksha Sannyasa Yoga, from the dialogue between Sri Krishna and Arjuna in the *Upanishad* known as *Shreemad Bhagavad Gita*, the science of the Absolute, the yoga shastra.

APPENDIX

PRONUNCIATION GUIDE OF SANSKRIT TRANSLITERATION ALPHABET

In this book, the Sanskrit verses of the *Bhagavad Gita* are presented as a transliterated version of the original Sanskrit text.

Sanskrit is usually written in an ancient Brahmic script, known as Devanagari, which has 49 primary characters:

- 14 vowels and 2 special letters (Table 1)
- 25 consonants divided in 5 groups (Table 2)
- 4 semi-vowels, 3 sibilants, 1 aspirate and 2 compounds (Table 3)

In contrast, the ISO (International Organisation for Standardisation) basic Latin alphabet consists only of 26 letters: 5 vowels and 21 consonants.

Therefore, when transliterating Devanagari into the Latin alphabet, it is necessary to use a combination of Latin letters and diacritics. The diacritics (also referred to as diacritical marks or diacritical signs) are symbols added to the Roman letters to indicate the extra sounds of the letters of the Sanskrit alphabet. The most common diacritical symbols used in Sanskrit transliteration are dashes, dots, accents, hyphens and tilde.

Several methods of Sanskrit transliteration have been developed since the Hunterian transliteration system was officially adopted by the Indian Government in the 1870s. Nowadays, the system most widely used is called IAST (International Alphabet of Sanskrit Transliteration), which was first introduced in the late 1890s.

In the tables shown in this guide, the IAST letters are listed as well as:

- the IPA (International Phonetic Alphabet)symbols, which represent the most similar English pronunciation to the sound of each IAST letter;

- examples of English words with similar sounds to the sound of each IAST letter;

- examples of Sanskrit words with each IAST letter;

- some notes about the characteristics of the Sanskrit sound of each IAST letter.

Each sound of the Sanskrit alphabet is made in one of five specific points of the vocal tract cavity, referred to as the five points of Sanskrit pronunciation (Diagram 1). Depending on the pronunciation point involved in the generation of the letter's sound, the letter is classified as Guttural, Palatal, Cerebral, Dental and Labial.

A Guttural letter is pronounced in the throat or near the back of the oral cavity. The Guttural letters are the vowels 'a' and 'ā' (Table 1); the 5 Guttural consonants 'k', 'kh', 'g', 'gh', and 'ṅ' (Table 2); and the aspirate 'h' (Table 3).

A Palatal letter is pronounced using the middle of the tongue against the back part of the roof of the mouth (soft palate). The Palatal letter are the vowels 'i' and 'ī' (Table 1); the 5 Palatal consonants 'c', 'ch', 'j', 'jh', and 'ñ' (Table 2); the semi-vowel 'y', and the sibilant 'ś' (Table 3).

A Cerebral letter is pronounced using the tip of the tongue against the front part of the roof of the mouth (hard palate). The Cerebral letters are the vowels 'ṛ' and 'ṝ' (Table 1); the 5 Cerebral consonants 'ṭ', 'ṭh', 'ḍ', 'ḍh', and 'ṇ' (Table 2); the semi-vowel 'r' and the sibilant 'ṣ' (Table 3).

A Dental letter is pronounced using the tip of the tongue against the top front teeth. The Dental letters are the 5 Dental consonants 't', 'th', 'd', 'dh', and 'n' (Table 2); the semi-vowel 'r' and the sibilant 'ṣ' (Table 3).

A Labial letter is pronounced using the lips. The Labial letters are the vowels 'u' and 'ū' (Table 1); the 5 Labial consonants 'p', 'ph', 'b', 'bh', and 'm' (Table 2); and the semi-vowel 'v' (Table 3).

The Sanskrit transliterated long vowels that are pronounced as diphthongs (Table 1) are classified as Guttural-Palatal ('ai') and Guttural-Labial ('au'), according to the letters that form the diphthong.

There are also 2 rare vowels, 'ḷ' and 'ḹ' (Table 1), which are classified as Cerebral-Dental, because they are first pronounced using the tip of the tongue against the top front teeth and then using the tip of the tongue against the roof of the mouth.

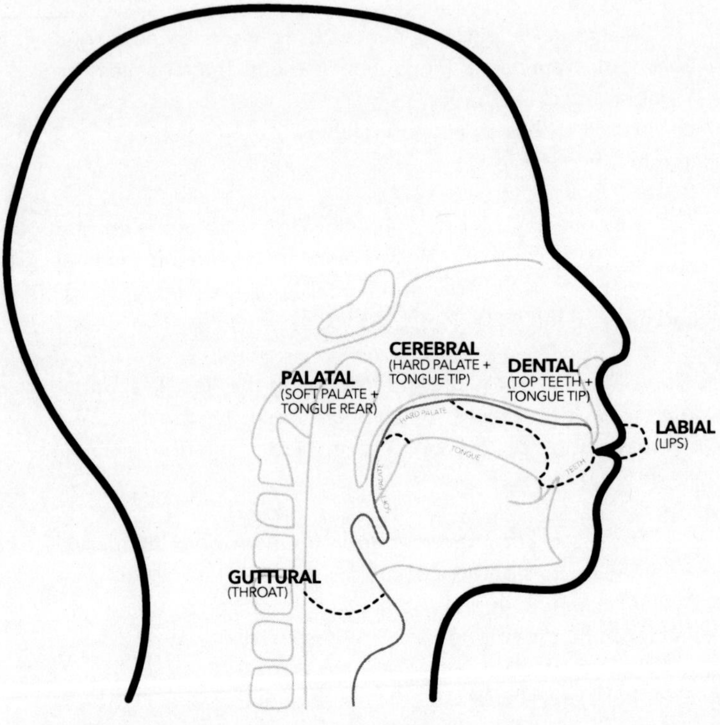

Diagram 1 – The five positions of the mouth and throat used for the pronunciation of the Sanskrit letters.

TABLE 1 - Pronunciation of the Sanskrit transliterated vowels (IAST).

VOWELS

IAST	IPA	ENGLISH (SIMILAR SOUNDS)	SANSKRIT WORDS	SANSKRIT SOUND
a	[ɐ] or [ə]	but, cut, hut, mother	arjuna, brahma	Guttural
ā	[ɑ:]	far, car, arm, father	āsana, pāṇḍava	Long vowel; twice as long as **a**
i	[i]	pin, bit, sit, outfit	siddha, kunti	Palatal
ī	[i:]	liter, need, beak, week	bhīṣma, gītā	Long vowel; twice as long as **i**
u	[u] or [ʊ]	push, put, book, foot	guru, duryodhan	Labial
ū	[u:]	rule, roof, tool, boot	pūjā, viśvarūpa	Long vowel; twice as long as **u**
ṛ	[ɹ̩]	rip, Rita, rich, pretty	Kṛṣṇa, kṛpā	Cerebral[1]
ṝ	[ɹ̩:]	reed	pitṝṇām, bhrātṝn	Long vowel; twice as long as **ṛ**
ḷ	-	lree, revelry	kḷp (root of 'kalpa')	Cerebral-Dental; very rare
ḹ	-	-	-	Long vowel; twice as long as **ḷ**
e	[e:]	they, grey, rate, cake	devī, bhūteṣu	Long vowel; Palatal
o	[o:]	go, boat, rope, hope	loka, gopāla	Long vowel; Labial
ai	[a:i]	aisle, bite, height, eye	vaiśyā, airāvata	Long vowel; Guttural-Palatal[2]
au	[a:u]	cow, now, how, sound	kaunteya, draupadī	Long vowel; Guttural-Labial[3]
ṁ	[ⁿ]	uncle, hum	ahiṁsā, saṁsāra	Anusvara[4]
ḥ	[h] or [x]	hot, home, aha, hue	duḥkha, kriyāḥ	Visarga[5]

Additional Notes:

1. The vowel 'ṛ' is pronounced with the tongue rolled slightly backward, pressing against the roof of the mouth. Often is pronounced as 'ri'.

2. Diphthong formed by the combination of 'a' and 'i', which is pronounced as the 'a' in 'sat', followed by 'i' as in 'pin'. However, very often the stress is on 'i' not on 'a'.

3. Diphthong formed by the combination of 'a' and 'u', which is pronounced as the 'a' in 'sat', followed by a 'u' as in 'put'. However, very often the stress is on 'u' not on 'a'.

4. Anusvara ('after-sound') it's a nasal sound pronounced through the nose with the mouth shut. It sounds as 'm' when it comes at the end of a word or before 'p', 'ph', 'b', 'bh', or 'm'. Otherwise, it's pronounced as 'n'.

5. Visarga ('sending-forth'): it's pronounced through emission of air. It sounds as 'h' in 'house', and at the end of the sentence it's followed by an echo of the preceding vowel (aḥ sounds as aha).

TABLE 2 – Pronunciation of the consonants (IAST).

CONSONANTS[1]

IAST	IPA	ENGLISH (SIMILAR SOUNDS)	SANSKRIT WORDS	SANSKRIT SOUND
CONSONANTS GUTTURALS				
k	[k]	kite, cook, kettle, call	karma, karuṇā	Unaspirated[2] hard[3] letter
kh	[kʰ]	inkhorn, Ekhart, blockhead	sukha, śikhaṇḍī	Aspirated hard letter
g	[g]	God, give, go, good	bhagavān, govinda	Unaspirated soft letter
gh	[gʰ]	bighead, doghouse	saṅgha, vyāghra	Aspirated soft letter
ṅ	[ŋ]	sing, bang, anger, tangled	sāṅkhya, ahaṅkāra	Nasal[4] soft letter
CONSONANTS PALATALS				
c	[c] or [t͡ɕ]	chair, catch, churn, chill	cakra, caraṇām	Unaspirated hard letter
ch	[cʰ] [t͡ɕʰ]	church-hat, staunch-heart	icchāmi, chittvā	Aspirated hard letter
j	[ɟ] or [d͡ʒ]	joy, jam, major, ajar	rajas, purujit, jīva	Unaspirated soft letter
jh	[ɟʰ] or [d͡ʒʰ]	hedgehog, bridgehead,	jhaṣāṇām, jhaṭiti	Aspirated soft letter
ñ	[ɲ]	canyon, Kenya, banyan	sañjaya, dhanañjaya	Nasal soft letter
CONSONANTS CEREBRALS				
ṭ	[ʈ]	tub, try, stick, tuck	aṣṭāṅga, dṛṣṭi	Unaspirated hard letter
ṭh	[ʈʰ]	blunthead, boathouse	pratiṣṭhā, niṣṭhā	Aspirated hard letter
ḍ	[ɖ]	dove, bird, deed, dig	paṇḍita, pāṇḍu	Unaspirated soft letter
ḍh	[ɖʰ]	red-hot, madhouse	mūḍha, suvirūḍha	Aspirated soft letter
ṇ	[ɳ]	cone, turn, phoned, land	prāṇa, nārāyaṇa	Nasal soft letter
CONSONANTS DENTALS				
t	[t]	teeth, pasta, together	tapas, tattva	Unaspirated hard letter
th	[t̪ʰ]	anthill, lighthouse	katha, pārtha	Aspirated hard letter
d	[d̪]	dive, dance, devotion	vidyā, pada	Unaspirated soft letter
dh	[d̪ʰ]	bloodhound, Godhood	dharma, dhyāna	Aspirated soft letter
n	[n]	nice, now, name, normal	āsana, namaḥ	Nasal soft letter
CONSONANTS LABIALS				
p	[p]	prince, paternal, primordial	pūjā, puruṣa	Unaspirated hard letter
ph	[pʰ]	uphill, loophole, upheaval	phalaṁ, phaleṣu	Aspirated hard letter
b	[b]	bliss, blessing, butter	buddhi, brahmacāri	Unaspirated soft letter
bh	[bʰ]	abhor, abhorrent	bhakti, bhārata	Aspirated soft letter
m	[m]	man, moon, met, aroma	mudrā, māyā	Nasal soft letter

Additional Notes:

1. It is important to note that the consonants of the Sanskrit transliteration alphabet need a vowel in order to be pronounced. So, they are often represented in a syllabic form, although not in this table, combined with 'a': 'ka', 'kha' etc.

2. In the Sanskrit alphabet there are 10 unaspirated consonants (k, g, c, j, ṭ, ḍ, t, d, p, b) and 10 aspirated consonants (kh, gh, ch, jh, ṭh, ḍh, th, dh, ph, bh). The aspirated consonants are pronounced in the same way as the correspondent unaspirated letter, but with an extra puff of air.

3. In the Sanskrit alphabet there are 10 hard consonants (k, kh, c, ch, ṭ, ṭh, t, th, p, ph) and 10 soft consonants (g, gh, j, jh, ḍ, ḍh, d, dh, b, bh). The hard consonants do not reverberate, which means that they are pronounced without vibration of the vocal cords, whereas the soft consonants do reverberate, so there is a re-echo of their sound.

4. The nasal consonants (ṅ, ñ, ṇ n, m) are pronounced by redirecting the flow of air through the nasal cavity. All the nasal consonants are soft letters.

TABLE 3 - Pronunciation of the Sanskrit transliterated semi-vowels, sibilants, aspirate and compounds (IAST).

IAST	IPA	ENGLISH (SIMILAR SOUNDS)	SANSKRIT WORDS	SANSKRIT SOUND
SEMI-VOWELS (SOFT)				
y	[j]	**y**et, **y**earning, pla**y**er	**y**oga, ācār**y**a	Palatal
r	[r] or [ɾ]	**r**un, **r**at, **r**athe**r**, d**r**ama	**r**āma, **r**ajas, p**r**ema	Cerebral[1]
l	[l]	**l**eaf, **l**ight, **l**ook, fai**l**ed	**l**okā, maṅga**l**aṁ	Dental[2]
v	[v] or [ʋ]	**v**ision, **v**ariety, e**v**er, **v**erse	**v**iṣṇu, **v**eda, **v**ākya	Labial[3]
SIBILANTS (HARD)				
ś	[ɕ]	**sh**ut, **sh**all, **sh**eep	**ś**ikhaṇḍī, **ś**rīmad	Palatal[4]
ṣ	[ʂ]	lea**sh**, ru**sh**, a**ss**ure, **sh**arp	ni**ṣ**ṭhā, puru**ṣ**a	Cerebral[5]
s	[s]	**s**un, **s**urf, **s**oft, **s**ell	**s**attva, **s**iddhi	Dental
ASPIRATE (SOFT)				
h	[ɦ]	**h**ello, **h**oly, a**h**ead, **h**at	**h**anumān, **h**ari	Guttural
COMPOUNDS				
kṣ	[kʂ]	a**c**tion, ba**cksh**ift	la**kṣ**mī, **kṣ**atriya	-
jñ	[ɟɲ]	I**gn**eous, ge**n**ious	**jñ**āna, ā**jñ**a, ya**jñ**a	-

Additional Notes:

1. The semi-vowel 'r' is pronounced with the tongue rolled slightly backward pressing against the front part of the roof of the mouth (hard palate). The sound is stronger than the English 'r.

2. The semi-vowel 'l' is pronounced as the 'l' in 'life' with the tip of the tongue fully pressing the back of the teeth.

3. The semi-vowel 'v' is pronounced as 'v' in 'vision', except when it appears after a consonant, where it may be pronounced as 'w', which sounds like 'u' in 'swami'.

4. The sibilant 'ś' is pronounced as 'sh' in 'shut' with the back of the tongue touching the back part of the roof of the mouth (soft palate), where the sound of the vowel 'eee' is made.

5. The sound of the sibilant 'ṣ' is similar to the sound of the sibilant ‹ś›, but it is pronounced with the tip of the tongue rolled slightly back, and pressing backward against the front part of the roof of the mouth (hard palate).

ABOUT PARAMAHAMSA SRI SWAMI VISHWANANDA

Paramahamsa Sri Swami Vishwananda is a fully realised spiritual Master, whose international mission, known as Bhakti Marga, 'the path of devotion', is based in the heart of Europe. He travels the world to encourage all people to recognise the universal Love that lies within each human being, and to awaken their innate ability to express that Love in their daily lives.

Effortlessly connecting principles of eastern spirituality with elements of western spiritual tradition, Paramahamsa Vishwananda reveals the underlying oneness of the Divine and inspires a unique experience of spirituality, regardless of culture, religion, gender or age.

Giving Darshans and Satsangs tirelessly throughout the year, Paramahamsa Vishwananda introduces these simple but profound concepts in a very personal way, answering questions about love, life, death, healing, and faith. In addition, his commentaries on supplementary Vedic texts and on the *Shreemad Bhagavad Gita*, one of the most popular sacred Hindu scriptures in the world, help a worldwide audience gain a deeper understanding of the universal messages they contain, and spread the message of love, peace and unity to all of mankind.

OTHER BOOKS BY PARAMAHAMSA VISHWANANDA

Shreemad Bhagavad Gita: The Song of Love – Commentary by Paramahamsa Sri Swami Vishwananda

The Essence of Shreemad Bhagavatam: A Seven-Day Journey to Love – Commentary by Paramahamsa Sri Swami Vishwananda

The Guru Gita: Commentary on the Great Mysteries of the Guru-disciple Relationship

Sri Gopi Gita: The Song of the Longing Hearts – Commentary by Paramahamsa Sri Swami Vishwananda

Hanuman Chalisa Bhasya

Inspiration: Timeless Stories of Divine Love

The Just Love Series:

- Just Love
- Just Love 2
- Just Love 3
- Just Love 1/2/3: Questions and Answers

OTHER BHAKTI MARGA PUBLICATIONS

Blossoming of the Heart

Unity with the Divine

Journey to Freedom

Christ Krishna

Bhakti Marga: A Decade of Love

To order these books, visit **publications.bhaktimarga.org**

Or go to **bhaktimarga.org** to find the Bhakti Marga centre nearest you.

Paramahamsa
Vishwananda

THE ESSENCE OF EVERYTHING IS
Just Love